Charles M. Schulz

The People to Know Series

Madeleine Albright
0-7660-1143-7

Ansel Adams
0-7660-1847-4

Neil Armstrong
0-89490-828-6

Isaac Asimov
0-7660-1031-7

Robert Ballard
0-7660-1147-X

Margaret Bourke-White
0-7660-1534-3

Garth Brooks
0-7660-1672-2

Barbara Bush
0-89490-350-0

Willa Cather
0-89490-980-0

Bill Clinton
0-89490-437-X

Hillary Rodham Clinton
0-89490-583-X

Bill Cosby
0-89490-548-1

Walt Disney
0-89490-694-1

Bob Dole
0-89490-825-1

Marian Wright Edelman
0-89490-623-2

Bill Gates
0-89490-824-3

Ruth Bader Ginsberg
0-89490-621-6

John Glenn
0-7660-1532-7

Jane Goodall
0-89490-827-8

Al Gore
0-7660-1232-8

Tipper Gore
0-7660-1142-9

Billy Graham
0-7660-1533-5

Alex Haley
0-89490-573-2

Tom Hanks
0-7660-1436-3

Ernest Hemingway
0-89490-979-7

Ron Howard
0-89490-981-9

Steve Jobs
0-7660-1536-X

Helen Keller
0-7660-1530-0

John F. Kennedy
0-89490-693-3

Stephen King
0-7660-1233-6

John Lennon
0-89490-702-6

Maya Lin
0-89490-499-X

Charles Lindbergh
0-7660-1535-1

Jack London
0-7660-1144-5

Malcolm X
0-89490-435-3

Wilma Mankiller
0-89490-498-1

Branford Marsalis
0-89490-495-7

Anne McCaffrey
0-7660-1151-8

Barbara McClintock
0-89490-983-5

Rosie O'Donnell
0-7660-1148-8

Gary Paulsen
0-7660-1146-1

Christopher Reeve
0-7660-1149-6

Ann Richards
0-89490-497-3

Sally Ride
0-89490-829-4

Will Rogers
0-89490-695-X

Franklin D. Roosevelt
0-89490-696-8

Charles M. Schulz
0-7660-1846-6

Steven Spielberg
0-89490-697-6

John Steinbeck
0-7660-1150-X

Martha Stewart
0-89490-984-3

Amy Tan
0-89490-699-2

Alice Walker
0-89490-620-8

Andy Warhol
0-7660-1531-9

Simon Wiesenthal
0-89490-830-8

Elie Wiesel
0-89490-428-0

Frank Lloyd Wright
0-7660-1032-5

People to Know

Charles M. Schulz

Cartoonist and Creator of Peanuts

Michael A. Schuman

Enslow Publishers, Inc.

40 Industrial Road   PO Box 38
Box 398   Aldershot
Berkeley Heights, NJ 07922 Hants GU12 6BP
USA   UK

http://www.enslow.com

To Blakeslee Lloyd, my high school writing teacher, who instilled in me the confidence to follow my dreams.

Library of Congress Cataloging-in-Publication Data

Schuman, Michael A.
    Charles M. Schulz : cartoonist and creator of Peanuts / Michael A. Schuman.
        p. cm. — (People to know)
    Includes bibliographical references and index.
    Summary: A biography of the artist whose "Li'l Folks" turned into the most successful comic strip of all time, "Peanuts," including how his characters reflected events in his own life.
    ISBN 0-7660-1846-6 (Hardcover)
    1. Schulz, Charles M.—Juvenile literature. 2. Cartoonists—United States—Biography—Juvenile literature. [1. Schulz, Charles M. 2. Cartoonists.] I. Title. II. Series.
    PN6727.S3 Z85 2002
    741.5'092—dc21
                                       2001004473

Printed in the United States of America

10 9 8 7 6 5 4 3 2

To Our Readers:
We have done our best to make sure all Internet Addresses in this book were active and appropriate when we went to press. However, the author and the publisher have no control over and assume no liability for the material available on those Internet sites or on other Web sites they may link to. Any comments or suggestions can be sent by e-mail to comments@enslow.com or to the address on the back cover.

Contents

Acknowledgments

Many thanks for all their time to Lynn Johnston, Cathy Guisewite, Bill Melendez, Clark Gesner, Derrick Bang, Linus Maurer, Dale Hale, Edna Poehner, Amy Lago, Haymme Marin, Craig Schulz, Monte Schulz, Amy Johnson, and Jill Schulz Transki.

Seven Newspapers

Twenty-seven-year-old Charles Schulz was becoming the railroad's best customer. It was 1950, and he was a struggling cartoonist trying to sell his comic strip *Li'l Folks*. Schulz's train travels took him to the offices of newspaper syndicates—companies that supply comics and other features to newspapers. Most of the major newspaper syndicates were located in cities much bigger than St. Paul, Minnesota, where Schulz lived. The closest syndicate was in Chicago, about four hundred miles away. Schulz often boarded the train with samples of his cartoons early in the morning, settling in for the long trip.

Sometimes he spoke to other passengers. Mostly he kept to himself, for he was a quiet and shy young man.[1] One time he mustered the courage to approach

Charles M. Schulz

a pretty girl on the train. He sat down next to her and asked if she liked the book she was reading. She said she did. Schulz could not think of anything else to say, so he got up and left. Making conversation can be awkward and difficult for some people—and Schulz was one of them. Understanding and portraying these feelings would become an important theme in his comic strips one day.

After his train arrived in Chicago, Schulz would visit the offices of different publications and syndicates to show his comics to the editors. Some were polite, but others rudely dismissed him. They were not interested in his work.

Back in St. Paul, Schulz spent his days working as a teacher at Art Instruction Schools, Inc., a correspondence school in St. Paul's twin city, Minneapolis. The art course was given through the mail. Schulz's students lived all over the country and sent in their completed assignments for him to grade. Schulz enjoyed his job, but he dreamed of being a full-time cartoonist.

Schulz also mailed samples of his comics to publications and syndicates based in cities farther away. In the spring of 1950, he sent his best drawings to United Feature Syndicate in New York City. After several weeks went by without a reply, Schulz thought his drawings might have been lost in the mail.[2] He wrote a letter asking about them, and Jim Freeman, the syndicate's editorial director, wrote back. He liked Schulz's samples and invited the cartoonist to New York to talk in person.

On a June day, Schulz boarded a train in St. Paul

bound for New York City. Upon arriving, he spent a night at the Roosevelt Hotel. When he awoke the next morning, the weather was dreary and rainy. Without stopping to eat breakfast, Schulz hurried over to the syndicate building. It was early, and none of the editors had arrived for work. Schulz handed the receptionist, Helyn Rippert, some of his newest drawings. Then he excused himself to grab a bite to eat.

When Schulz returned from breakfast, he found the syndicate editors looking over his latest comic strips. They liked the new ones even better than the earlier drawings. Syndicate president Larry Rutman was so excited about the new comic strip that he was ready to give Schulz a deal right then and there.

Rutman offered Schulz a five-year contract to draw his comic strip for United Feature Syndicate. Schulz and the syndicate would split profits fifty-fifty. The syndicate would own the copyright.[3] That means it would have the rights to produce, sell, and distribute the comic strip. Schulz gladly accepted. "I remember thinking, 'Now I'm a cartoonist, not just an instructor at a correspondence school,'" he said later.[4]

On October 2, 1950, *Peanuts* ran for the first time. There were several thousand daily newspapers in the United States then. *Peanuts* appeared in a grand total of seven.[5] Who could have known that this was the start of what many people would consider the most successful comic strip in the history of the world?

Needles, Sketches, and a Dog Named Spike

Charles Monroe Schulz was born in Minneapolis, Minnesota, on November 26, 1922. Just two days later, an uncle nicknamed him after, of all things, a comic strip character. A horse named Spark Plug had just been introduced into a popular comic called *Barney Google*. From that day on, Charles Schulz would be known to his friends as Sparky.

The reason baby Charles was given that nickname has long been forgotten, though it is known that many members of his family were big fans of the daily and Sunday comics.[1] Sparky's father, Carl, was a barber who owned the Family Barber Shop in St. Paul, Minnesota. Sparky's mother, Dena, was a homemaker. Schulz later said that his talent was not inherited

Sparky's parents, Carl and Dena Schulz.

from any relatives: "There were no artists in the family, but there were a lot of funny people."[2]

Young Sparky loved to draw, and he was good at it. One day in kindergarten his teacher handed out black crayons and white paper and told the children to draw whatever they wanted. Sparky drew a picture of a man shoveling snow, a common scene in Minnesota, where the winters are long and cold. Then he added a palm tree. His teacher looked at the picture and told him, "Someday, Charles, you're going to be an artist."[3]

As a boy, Sparky walked to the nearest drugstore every Saturday evening to buy the Sunday feature sections of the two Minneapolis newspapers. He and his father liked to read them together. On Sunday mornings, the two newspapers from neighboring St. Paul were delivered to the stores, and Sparky would buy those as well. He and his father then had four comic sections to amuse themselves. They liked everything from the adventurous *Buck Rogers* to the slapstick *Krazy Kat.* Sparky had no brothers or sisters, so his father was his reading buddy for the funnies, or funny pages, as they were called then.

Sparky also liked playing sports, especially baseball and ice hockey. Like almost all the children in Minnesota at that time, Sparky learned to skate at an early age. The children skated on patches of ice that formed in their backyards, in parks, and in front of their schools. There were no indoor skating rinks back then, but he found a way to practice indoors. Using a hockey stick, he hit tennis balls toward a goal he had set up in the basement. His grandmother

Sparky liked riding around on his tricycle.

played goaltender, using a broom to protect the goal. "She made a lot of great saves," Schulz later recalled.[4]

After Sparky finished first grade, his parents moved far from the frigid climate of Minnesota. They packed their belongings into their 1928 Ford and headed southwest. Sparky squeezed onto the back-seat with his pet Boston bull terrier, Snooky, as his parents drove the dirt and gravel roads that laced the land in those early days of road building. Their destination was the dusty desert community of Needles, California.

Needles is a lonely town on the California-Arizona border, about 260 miles northeast of Los Angeles. Sparky never understood why his family made the move. His father, Carl, was a homebody who did not like changes in his daily routine. Such a major move was out of character.

The Schulzes had relatives who had already moved to Needles. One was Sparky's teenage cousin, Howard, who had been diagnosed with tuberculosis. The disease caused bacterial growths on his lungs. One symptom is difficulty breathing. Today there is a vaccination to prevent tuberculosis. At that time, people thought a dry climate helped lessen its symptoms.

As he had in Minnesota, Carl Schulz worked as a barber. He cut customers' hair in a downtown Needles building he shared with his wife's brother, Monroe, who was also a barber. As for Sparky, he entered second grade as the new kid in town and proved to be a very good student. When the school year ended, he and a girl named Marie Holland had earned awards as the most outstanding students in their class.

Carl, Dena, and Sparky Schulz stayed in Needles a little more than a year. Then they returned to St. Paul, and Carl went back to work in his old barbershop. Times were tough during the 1930s, a period known as the Great Depression. At the Depression's peak, 25.2 percent of the workers in the United States were unemployed.[5] Millions of Americans were homeless. Even those who had a place to live often wondered where their next meal would come from.

The Schulzes were lucky. People needed to get their hair cut, so Carl always had business. He commonly worked ten to thirteen hours a day, six days a week. The family lived a short distance from the barbershop, and Sparky often strolled over in the evening. He would wait for his father to finish work, then the two would walk home together.

When it came time for Sparky to get a haircut, his father was right there with clippers and comb in hand. If an important customer came into the shop before his father had finished with Sparky, Carl would ask his son to kindly step aside and wait. "I was always terribly embarrassed having to sit on the bench with a half-finished haircut," Schulz later recalled.[6]

Sparky continued to excel in school. He was so bright that he skipped the second half of third grade, finishing out the school year in fourth grade. He later skipped the second half of fifth grade. Sometimes during school he would doodle and sketch on his notebooks. He often drew cartoon characters such as Mickey Mouse and Popeye. Other children admired

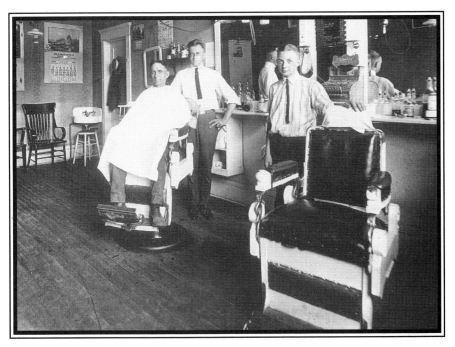

Carl Schulz, the barber at the left chair, and his brother-in-law, Monroe Halverson, right, shared a barbershop.

his work and many asked him to make the same drawings on their notebooks.

Outside school he continued playing sports. Baseball became his favorite pastime. There were no organized leagues, so Sparky and his friends formed their own teams and played on vacant lots. Many of these places had no backstops, and the kids chased foul balls into the street. When a ball rolled down a storm drain, as often happened, someone would have to be lowered inside to retrieve it.

Sparky also enjoyed going to the movies on Saturdays at the Park Theater, which was just half a block from his father's barbershop. The theaters at that time showed short films before the main feature. Sparky enjoyed a serial called *Rin Tin Tin*, which was an adventure series about a boy and his dog. One Saturday, the Park Theater ran a special promotion to draw children. The first hundred kids who bought tickets that day would receive a free Butterfinger candy bar. As luck would have it, Sparky was number 101 in line.

Because he had been moved ahead two grades in elementary school, Sparky entered junior high as the smallest and youngest student in the school. He became very shy and his grades began to suffer. He received his first failing mark in seventh-grade arithmetic. One girl saw the failing grade on his report card, and she and a friend laughed out loud at him. Sparky was having so much trouble he was kept back in eighth grade. That did not help. In high school his grades were even worse. In ninth grade he flunked algebra. The next year he failed both Latin and English.

Sparky was too shy to join the school art club, and he ate lunch by himself. He never asked a girl out on a date. A tall, thin boy with pimples and big ears, he thought no girl would want to go out with him.[7] "I wasn't actually hated," Schulz later said. "Nobody cared that much."[8]

As an adult, Schulz often thought about his failures in school: "The astounding part, as I look back upon it, is that no one ever said anything. Not one teacher ever called me to her desk and said, 'What seems to be the problem, Charles?'"[9]

Sparky's dog Spike was so smart that he understood more than fifty words. Years later, Spike's personality inspired Charles Schulz to create Snoopy.

While in high school, Sparky had one major success: He had a cartoon published in Ripley's *Believe It or Not!* This popular one-panel comic of the day featured illustrations of oddities in the world, such as a full-sized building made of paper or a two-headed calf. Most of the drawings and text were created by cartoonist Robert Ripley, but Ripley also accepted submissions from the public.

Sparky sent in an illustration of his black-and-white mixed-breed dog Spike, who seemed to eat just about anything. Sparky's drawing ran in Ripley's *Believe It or Not!* on February 22, 1937, with the caption "A hunting dog that eats pins, tacks and razor blades is owned by C. F. Schulz, St. Paul, Minn." (The letter *F* rather than *M* was mistakenly printed as Schulz's middle initial.) The credit read, "Drawn by Sparky."[10]

In his junior year of high school, Sparky flunked physics with a grade of zero.[11] He later joked, "I think I'm the worst physics student in the history of Central High School."[12]

Sparky began to master the game of golf, and he did make his high school's golf team. Typically, though, he lost the only important match he played. He then lost the consolation round, too. This experience helped him understand what it was like to disappoint at sports.

By his senior year, Sparky began to buckle down and work harder in school. He received A's and B's throughout the year and was so proud that he saved his report card for the rest of his life. His favorite course was illustration. "It was probably the only few months when I ever enjoyed school," he said later.[13]

Sparky's illustration teacher, Minette Paro, encouraged his work. Paro once gave the class an assignment to draw small objects in groups of three. Sparky covered the paper with trios of all sorts, including golf clubs, traffic signals, telephones, and paint brushes. Paro recalled, "They were spectacular because they were things that you wouldn't even think of. That means that his mind is working every minute."[14]

As Sparky's senior year in high school was winding down, Paro suggested that he submit some cartoons to the high school yearbook. Sparky happily did so and looked forward to seeing them published.[15] On

Sparky was only fifteen years old when his drawing of Spike appeared in Ripley's Believe It or Not!

the last day of school, he grabbed his copy of the yearbook and tore through the pages looking for his illustrations. They were nowhere to be found. Sparky's drawings had been rejected, and he never learned why.[16]

Schulz later said, "I was so glad when I graduated from high school. The whole experience was miserable, and I was just glad to get out. I hated being made a fool of, and I hated not knowing what was going on. But it was my own fault. I didn't work hard enough. I hated homework, and I was extremely immature. All I was interested in were art and golf."[17]

". . . Doing Something with Cartoons"

Shortly after Schulz graduated from high school, his mother showed him an ad for Federal Schools (later called Art Instruction Schools, Inc.). It said, "Do you like to draw? Send in for our free talent test."[1]

Schulz enrolled in illustration courses. Living in a neighboring city, Schulz could have brought his drawings in person to the school to be graded. Instead, he sent them in by mail, for he had doubts whether the work he did was good.[2] Money was still hard to come by and his father had trouble paying the bills for the school tuition. Yet Carl Schulz told his son not to worry. He would always find a way to pay for his son's schooling.

Schulz completed the course, but his grades were

not outstanding. In the subject of drawing children, Schulz was given a C-minus. The teacher thought he was a little worse than average in that skill.

Still, Schulz continued to draw cartoons. He sent his best ones to magazines across the country in hopes that someone would buy one. He had no luck and succeeded only in collecting piles of rejection slips. Schulz earned some money by taking odd jobs. One was at a direct mail advertising company in downtown Minneapolis. Although Schulz was hired as a "junior artist," he spent hardly any of his time drawing. Most of the time he just made deliveries. He learned that the boss often took advantage of young artists by hiring them to do these menial tasks.

Schulz took two more similar jobs before being hired to work in a mail room at another direct mail advertising firm, Associated Letter Service. He got along well with the six other young coworkers. They shared laughs while addressing labels or tying bundles, and Schulz said that he "discovered the wonderful feeling for the first time in my life of being liked."[3]

It also turned out to be the first time he got paid to draw and to letter text on a regular basis. The company's owners realized that this mail room worker had talent, and they asked him to illustrate some of their brochures. Away from work, however, there was sadness in the Schulz home. Dena Schulz was suffering from cancer. Both father and son did their best to cope with Dena's illness.

Schulz did not choose his next job. World War II was raging overseas, and in February 1943 Schulz, like thousands of other American men, was drafted into the army. His first stop was an induction center at Fort Snelling, not far from St. Paul. After two weeks at Fort Snelling, the budding cartoonist went home for a weekend to visit his parents. As Schulz's brief visit home was coming to a close, his mother said, "Well, I suppose we should say goodbye, Sparky, because we'll probably never see each other again."[4]

Sadly, her prediction came true. Dena Schulz died the next day. "It was a crushing blow to a kid," Schulz said. "Suddenly she's gone, and the next thing I know, after the funeral, I'm on a troop train roaring through the night to Fort Campbell, Kentucky, and basic [training]. Getting shots. Trooping into the mess hall for breakfast in the middle of the night. Eating things I'd never seen before."[5]

Schulz's first weeks in the army were horribly lonely, and he cried in his bunk at night. In time, though, he was able to move past his mother's death. He began training as a machine gunner and became adept at handling a weapon. He earned the rank of staff sergeant and was leader of a light machine gun squad. Although he later served in France and in southern Germany, Schulz saw little action. He had only one chance to use his gun, and that was in the last week of the war in Europe. While traveling along a road in a motorized vehicle called a half-track, Schulz saw a German soldier in a field. He aimed at the German and pulled the trigger. Nothing happened. Schulz had forgotten to load the weapon. Luckily, the soldier raised his hands over his head and surrendered.

In the army, Schulz learned how it felt to be lonely. These feelings later found a voice in his comic strip.

On another occasion he was about to lob a grenade into a German artillery emplacement when he saw a stray dog wander inside. Even though there might have been German soldiers there, Schulz refused to throw the grenade, for it would have meant certain death for a harmless animal. Thankfully, no one was inside the emplacement. Schulz said, "I guess I fought a pretty civilized war."[6]

Schulz was released from the army when the war in Europe ended in 1945. The young veteran was proud of his success as machine gun squad leader, but after a while his old insecurities kicked in. "I came home with a good feeling about myself, which lasted about twenty minutes," he said.[7]

Schulz moved with his father into a small apartment above his father's barbershop at the corner of Snelling and Selby Avenues in St. Paul. He began to draw again and applied for a job lettering tombstones. However, he never received a return call from that company. He did end up with a lettering job—but one of a much different kind. It was for a company called Timeless Topix, owned by the Roman Catholic Church. Timeless Topix published comic magazines with religious themes. Schulz's job was to write the letters for cartoons drawn and written by others. He even lettered French and Spanish translations, although he did not speak either language. He simply copied what was written down in front of him.

Not long afterward, Schulz took a second job, working days at Art Instruction Schools, Inc. For a year he spent his evenings lettering Timeless Topix cartoons, sometimes staying up well past midnight to finish. Early the next morning he would ride the streetcar to downtown St. Paul, where he would drop off his work at the Timeless Topix office. Then another streetcar would deliver him to downtown Minneapolis and his job at the correspondence school. Although he kept a busy schedule and was lacking in sleep, Schulz had no complaints. He said, "I regarded it as something great. I was involved. I was doing something with cartoons."[8]

One of his coworkers at the art school was a man named Charlie Brown. The men became good friends. Another teacher, who sat next to Schulz, was Linus Maurer. Recalling those days, Maurer said, "Sparky was happy to be working there. We had a wonderful group of teachers. We worked hard and had a lot of fun. There was a lot of banter and funny chitchat, and we pulled funny pranks on each other. It was a wonderful teaching environment."[9]

One day, as a practical joke, Maurer placed a fake parking ticket on the windshield of Schulz's car. As they were standing by the school window, Maurer called Schulz's attention to it. When Schulz saw the ticket, said Maurer, "he moaned and groaned about it. Then later, when we went out to lunch, I planned to show him it wasn't a real ticket. But since the time we had looked out the window, the meter maid had come by. She gave everyone tickets but Sparky. She thought the paper on his windshield was a real ticket. But everyone else had one, including me."[10]

Among the other staff at the correspondence school was a young woman named Frieda Rich. "She was from Canada," Maurer said, "and was an artist who worked as an instructor. Her hair was very curly. She curled it obviously, but she'd be sarcastic and say, 'How do you like my naturally curly hair?'"[11]

Another instructor, Frank Wing, was a cartoonist who had illustrated a feature comic strip, *Yesterdays*, in the 1930s. Wing was an expert at realistic drawings and taught Schulz the importance of drawing objects accurately.

Schulz also began enjoying the company of another staff member. Donna Mae Johnson was not an art instructor but worked in the school's accounting department. She was a small young woman with blue eyes and bright red hair. She and Schulz liked to leave notes on each other's desks. Donna decided to join the art school's softball team for one reason: Sparky Schulz was the coach. They began seeing more of each other outside work. Sometimes they went to dinner and a movie. Other times they would see a live show like the Ice Capades or perhaps a hockey game.

At the same time, Donna was dating another young man. Al Wold was also a World War II veteran. Both Sparky and Al were in love with Donna, and she was in love with both men. They wanted to marry her, and she knew she would soon have to decide between the two. One would become her husband and the other would have his heart broken.

From *Li'l Folks* to *Peanuts*

4

While Schulz and Donna Johnson were dating, he was making a determined effort to sell his cartoons. He sent them to magazines and syndicates around the country. Cartoonist Frank Wing thought Schulz's best drawings were those of little children and suggested that he concentrate on them. The younger cartoonist respected his friend and took Wing's advice seriously.

Schulz tried to mail at least one submission every week. Finally, all those trips to the post office paid off. In 1947 his hometown newspaper, the *St. Paul Pioneer Press*, agreed to run *Li'l Folks* every Sunday as a regular series. The newspaper grouped four different single-panel cartoons in a box that ran two columns

Sparky and Donna Mae Johnson in 1950: Schulz's girlfriend Donna would enter his comic strip one day as "the little red-haired girl."

wide. The *Li'l Folks* cartoons featured kids only. No adults were ever shown.

Like many single-panel cartoons, *Li'l Folks* did not run on the comic pages, which were reserved mostly for multipanel strips. *Li'l Folks* was printed in what was then called the women's section, along with articles about food, columns about raising children, and wedding announcements. Schulz's first *Li'l Folks* effort appeared in the December 7, 1947, issue of the *Pioneer Press*.

Most of the *Li'l Folks* cartoons featured a child saying something cute in an everyday situation. In one cartoon, two babies are sitting next to each other in high chairs. One baby says, "I find that this high altitude does wonders for my appetite."[1] Another panel shows two small boys sitting on a bench at a hockey game. One boy, mouth wide open, exclaims, "Wow! That's the third penalty they've given Grandma for unnecessary roughness."[2] That punch line was inspired by Schulz's boyhood days of practicing hockey with his grandmother in the basement.

Around that time, Schulz sent a cartoon to *The Saturday Evening Post*, a famous national magazine. It showed a little boy perched at the end of a long lounge chair, stretching his feet onto the footstool. The cartoon is funny because it captures children's desires to try to act grown up. Here was a little boy who had more than enough room to lean his back against the chair, stretch out, and be comfortable. But he wanted to use a footstool like a grown-up. So he sat awkwardly at the end of the lounge just so his feet would reach the stool. There was no caption with the cartoon, and the boy did not have a name. However, he did look a bit like the character who would become Schroeder in *Peanuts*.

Some weeks later Schulz found a note in his mailbox from *The Saturday Evening Post:* "Check Tuesday for spot drawing of little boy on chaise lounge."[3] Schulz was so used to rejection slips, he thought the note meant that he should check Tuesday's mail, when he would receive the cartoon back. Instead he got a check for $40, and his cartoon appeared in *The Saturday Evening Post* on May 29, 1948.

These were happy years for the young Minnesotan.[4] He was taking giant steps toward a career by selling some cartoons. He had a girlfriend he was in love with. And he was learning a lot from Frank Wing and other experienced cartoonists at the correspondence school.

After *Li'l Folks* had run continuously for two years on the women's page, Schulz decided to ask the newspaper for more money. The editor said no. Could *Li'l Folks* could be moved from the women's page to the Sunday comics page? asked Schulz. Again, the answer was no. Frustrated, Schulz said that maybe he should just quit drawing *Li'l Folks* altogether. The editor replied, simply, "OK, let's drop it."[5] And that was the end of *Li'l Folks*. The last comic ran on January 22, 1950.

Schulz still had *The Saturday Evening Post* as a backup. He eventually sold seventeen cartoons to the magazine.[6] The last one was published on July 8, 1950. By then Schulz had sold the rights to his characters

At last! Schulz was delighted to sell some of his cartoons.

to United Feature Syndicate, and he directed his efforts toward his new comic strip.

Early in the summer of 1950, Schulz asked Donna Johnson to marry him. She was not ready to answer, so Schulz gave her a little cat ornament that was to be used as a signal. Donna kept it in a desk drawer at work. When she was ready to say yes to marriage, she was to find an occasion when Schulz was not at his desk. Then she would place the cat atop it.

Schulz had no idea that on July 1, Al Wold also proposed to Donna. On a late July afternoon, Sparky and Donna got together one last time. As they sat on the back steps of her house, she told Sparky that she had said yes to Al. Schulz drove away, and she went inside her house and cried. Schulz came back a half hour later and asked if she had changed her mind. She had not.

Donna Johnson then quit her job at the correspondence school. It would have been awkward to continue working at the same place as Schulz. Years later Johnson said, "That was a terrible decision to have to make, because I really loved both Al and Sparky. . . . It was not easy. It was not easy."[7]

Why did Johnson decide to marry Al Wold? She thought perhaps it was because they had known each other since the eighth grade and had more or less grown up together.[8] They also had many mutual friends and attended the same church.

To Sparky Schulz, this rejection was tougher than any he had ever faced before. He admitted, "I didn't deal with it very well. I dreamed about it for years . . .

but I've made use of it all, of course."[9] Schulz's life crises fueled many of his comic strips.

Although his heart was broken, Schulz was making great progress in his work. United Feature Syndicate was busy arranging for the publication of Schulz's new comic strip. Then Schulz learned that he would not be able to continue using the name *Li'l Folks*. A cartoonist named Tack Knight had the rights to a similar title, *Little Folks*. So Schulz and the editors at United Feature had to think of something new.

Schulz had already decided to name his main character after his coworker Charlie Brown. He pitched *Charlie Brown* and *Good Old Charlie Brown* as possible titles. Both were nixed by the syndicate editors. United Feature's production manager Bill Anderson was asked to come up with some suggestions for this new comic strip about kids. Anderson wrote down ten possibilities. One was *Peanuts*, which was slang for little children.

Schulz hated the name. In fact, when he heard that *Peanuts* had been chosen, he called syndicate president Larry Rutman. It was a horrible title for his comic strip, said Schulz, calling it "undignified, inappropriate, and confusing."[10] No one ever referred to kids as "peanuts," he insisted. Besides, readers would think "Peanuts" was the name of one of the characters.

Rutman said it was too late to change the name. The syndicate sales staff was ready to sell the comic strip to newspapers—and the syndicate editors believed it was a catchy title. Schulz was new in the business, and he lacked the power to argue. He worried that if he strongly challenged the name, the syndicate might just tell him to forget it. That had happened just a year earlier with *Li'l Folks* and the *St. Paul Pioneer Press* editor. So Schulz gave in.

Some cartoonists later questioned whether Schulz really did hate the name. They said that Schulz rejected it mainly because he did not think of it himself. Schulz's friend Linus Maurer disagrees. "I can confirm in my dialogue with Sparky that he never liked *Peanuts*," said Maurer. "He would have preferred another title. I gather that he felt 'peanuts' was an insignificant kind of thing. It's like if we're talking and I say, 'I have an idea that isn't worth peanuts,' or 'You've got twenty dollars and that's just peanuts.'"[11]

Peanuts first appeared on October 2, 1950, with a cast of four characters: Charlie Brown; his dog, Snoopy; a boy named Shermy, named after one of Schulz's childhood pals; and a girl named Patty. (This Patty was not the same character as Peppermint Patty, who would not appear until the mid-1960s.)

The strip published on that early fall day featured Shermy, Patty, and Charlie Brown. In the first frame, Shermy and Patty are sitting on a roadside curb and Charlie Brown is in the distance walking toward them. Shermy says to Patty, "Well! Here comes ol' Charlie Brown!" In the second frame, Charlie Brown walks past them as Shermy continues, "Good ol' Charlie Brown. . . . Yes, sir!" In the third frame, Charlie Brown is walking away from the two kids, and Shermy says once more, "Good ol' Charlie Brown . . ."

In the fourth and final frame, Shermy says with disgust, "How I hate him!"[12]

Snoopy made his first appearance two days later, on October 4, 1950.

A total of nineteen days after the *Peanuts* debut, Schulz's former sweetheart, Donna Mae Johnson, married Al Wold in a Lutheran church in Minneapolis. Schulz, meanwhile, had begun dating another woman. She was an attractive, blond-haired, blue-eyed sister of a coworker at the correspondence school. Her name was Joyce Halverson. (She was not related to Schulz's uncle Monroe Halverson.)

"Why Don't You Wish for Some Wings?"

In the first *Peanuts* comic strips, Snoopy and Charlie Brown looked different from the characters that appear today. They acted differently, too. Snoopy was smaller, more of a puppy than a full-grown beagle. Charlie Brown had a round head—and it was really big. In fact, all three human characters in the early days of the strip—Charlie Brown, Lucy, and Linus—had huge heads. Charlie Brown wore a solid-white T-shirt. Just ten weeks later, on December 21, Charlie Brown made his first appearance in the zigzag shirt that became his trademark top.

Although some readers believe Charlie Brown is bald, Schulz always said the boy has very fine, light-colored hair. Schulz gave Charlie Brown a round head

Schulz, left, immortalized the name of his friend and coworker Charlie Brown, right. Then Schulz reached into his own memories and experiences to bring the character to life.

to make him look very ordinary. The cartoonist thought his own face was so ordinary that people would not recognize him if they saw him outside his home or school. He transferred those feelings to Charlie Brown's appearance.[1]

Also, the original Charlie Brown was not yet a lovable loser. He was playful and in some ways a wise guy. In one early strip Patty asks if he thinks she's beautiful. Teasingly, he replies that she is getting older but maybe if he looks through half-closed eyes, he might like the way she looks. She scowls and begins chasing him. In the final frame, he runs from her, smiling, with the exit line, "It's risky, but I get my laughs."[2] It would be out of character for today's worried and insecure Charlie Brown to make such a comment.

Snoopy did not yet have a crazy fantasy life. He acted like any family pet. In one early strip Charlie Brown thinks Snoopy is howling at the moon until he realizes he is standing on Snoopy's paw. In another, Snoopy is given a cake on his birthday, with a hot dog in place of a candle.

In the real world of 1950, *Peanuts* gave no sign of becoming a success. One of the original seven newspapers, *The Seattle Times*, dropped it within three months. A few months later, *The Denver Post*, another of the first seven, let it go. Within a year, United Feature Syndicate's sales staff sold *Peanuts* to about ten more newspapers, but that was well below expectations. When sales manager Harry Gilburt was scolded by his bosses for poor sales, he said there were too many characters, and readers had trouble keeping track of them. Newspaper editors in 1950 were not used to a comic strip without a central character, Gilburt later explained.

Still, Gilburt believed in the strip. He came up with an idea to promote *Peanuts* to the newspaper editors and the confused readers. Newspapers were given small advertisements introducing each member of the *Peanuts* crew. Gilburt's idea worked. Within months, sales began to take off. *Peanuts* was on its way to becoming a hit.

In 1951 the first new character was added to *Peanuts*. On February 7, a girl named Violet introduces herself to Snoopy while Charlie Brown stands behind him. Dark-haired, with braids, she was the neighborhood's pretty girl. After Violet tells Snoopy her name and says how cute he is, Charlie Brown clears his throat and utters, "Ahem!!" In the last frame, Violet has gone. Charlie Brown growls at Snoopy, "Well, why didn't you introduce me?!"[3]

Schulz's life was changing fast. After dating for several months, he and Joyce Halverson were married on April 18, 1951. After the wedding, they moved into a house Carl Schulz was renting in St. Paul. By this time Carl had remarried. His house was big enough for his son and new daughter-in-law to share. Schulz turned the basement into a makeshift studio and worked at a card table drawing his comic strip.

Shortly afterward, on May 30, 1951, the first baby was seen in *Peanuts*. Schulz named him Schroeder after a boy he knew when the two worked as golf caddies. On the day Schroeder first appears in the comic strip as Patty's next-door neighbor, Patty tells Charlie

Brown to say something to him. Flustered, Charlie Brown simply spits out, "I don't know what to say . . . I always feel so uncomfortable near children!"[4]

Joyce Schulz was an adventurous person and welcomed changes in her life. She persuaded her husband to move from Minnesota to Colorado Springs, Colorado. Schulz tried working out of his house in Colorado, as he had in St. Paul. But there were too many distractions. When he could not come up with ideas, Schulz would get up from his drawing board and tackle household chores. He decided to rent an office in downtown Colorado Springs, where he could be alone. The office was small, and Schulz did not even have a telephone. Since he did not know anybody in town, he usually ate lunch by himself.

The first *Peanuts* Sunday comic strip was published on January 6, 1952. It ran in forty newspapers. Schulz, meanwhile, was not happy in his new home, so he decided to move his family back to St. Paul. They had spent about one year in Colorado.

The *Peanuts* neighborhood was changing, too, as new characters were introduced. Lucy joined the gang on March 3, 1952. Like the other characters, she had not yet developed the personality she would later be known for. And like the others, her appearance differed from the one readers would later recognize. She had bangs and big round circles for eyes. After editor Jim Freeman suggested that Schulz do away with Lucy's round eyes, the cartoonist replaced them with small black dots.

Then, on September 19, Lucy's brother Linus

made his debut. Like Schroeder, he entered the world of *Peanuts* as a baby who did not walk or talk.

Parenting offered a rich source of ideas for the cartoonist. Before long, the Schulzes had two small children, Meredith and baby Charles Monroe Schulz, Jr., nicknamed Monte. One day Schulz bought his daughter a toy piano. Of course, all Meredith could do was bang out a few plink-plank sounds. Seeing her pound on the piano gave Schulz an idea. What if a baby sat down at a toy piano and played beautiful music? That could be very funny!

One day in the strip Charlie Brown introduces Schroeder to a toy piano. He tells the baby, "The piano is a beautiful instrument if played properly."[5] The only sounds Charlie Brown can muster from the little piano are the typical plink, plink, plinks. Schroeder then sits down and plays like a concert pianist. The reader knows this by the real musical notes hovering in a thought bubble over the piano. As he watches Schroeder, Charlie Brown's big, round face clouds with embarrassment.

For several days following, *Peanuts* featured Schroeder at his piano, impressing the rest of the cast with the music of Brahms or Beethoven. In one strip, Charlie Brown picks up Schroeder and carries him over to a real piano. Schroeder sits on the big piano bench and sobs. The last frame shows Schroeder playing happily at his toy piano. Charlie Brown exclaims, "I don't get it . . . I just don't get it."[6]

Schroeder soon began to play Beethoven almost exclusively. Why did the little pianist like Beethoven so much? "My favorite composer is Brahms—I could listen to him all day—but Brahms isn't a funny word, Beethoven is," said Schulz.[7] The cartoonist also prided himself on accuracy. If he drew music in the strip when Schroeder was playing, he made certain the musical score was real.

That drive for accuracy led to another big move up in Schulz's career. One day an editor for the book publishing company Holt, Rinehart and Winston noticed a comic strip of a little boy in a striped shirt playing a toy piano. Thanks to Schulz's faithful copying of the music, the editor recognized that it was a Beethoven sonata. He had never read *Peanuts* before, but this caused him to start. Soon he was enjoying Charlie Brown and his friends so much that he decided the comic strips should be collected in a book.

In 1952, the first *Peanuts* book, simply titled *Peanuts*, was published. It included most of the comic strips from the first year and a half. Schulz did not want all his comic strips in the book. Those he did not think were funny or well drawn were left out. At the same time, some *Peanuts* strips were also reproduced in comic books published by United Feature Syndicate. These came out regularly and were sold at newsstands and other stores.

As the strip was growing, so was the Schulz family. Over the next couple of years, Charles and Joyce Schulz had a son, Craig, and a daughter, Amy. Then, on July 13, 1954, another little character entered the *Peanuts* cartoon cast: a boy in overalls who was covered with dirt. Patty sees him playing in the sand and asks his name. He says he does not have a name but people call him things. And what do they call him

Schulz believed that Charlie Brown's round head made him look very ordinary.

most? wonders Patty. "Pig-Pen," replies the boy. From then on, he appeared in *Peanuts* as the happily messy boy who always stood out from the crowd.

That year another book of daily comic strips was published by Holt, Rinehart and Winston, Inc. By this time the characters were starting to take on distinct personalities, sometimes culled from Schulz's home life. Charles and Joyce Schulz called their daughter Meredith a fussbudget. The cartoonist applied that quality to Lucy, who became the crabby know-it-all of the *Peanuts* characters. In one 1954 Sunday strip,

Lucy kicks Linus's cookie box and growls, "That's what I think of your box of cookies!" In the next frame she boots Schroeder's piano across the room and screams, "That's what I think of your ol' piano." She then kicks Patty's crayons, Shermy's marbles, Violet's stamp collection, and Charlie Brown's jigsaw puzzle. In the last frame, as her angry friends chase her away, she whines, "I'm frustrated and inhibited and nobody understands me."[8]

Charlie Brown had evolved into an unpopular worrier. In a 1954 strip he tells Lucy that he wishes he had a friend. "Why don't you just wish for some wings?" she says.[9] Violet and Patty were now best friends whose main purpose in life was to insult Charlie Brown. Lucy was in love with Schroeder, who paid no attention to her. Snoopy had not yet become so humanlike, but he was acting less like an ordinary dog. He could understand the comments of the children around him.

Linus was gradually growing up. On June 1, 1954, comic readers for the first time saw him curled up with his special blanket. Some of Schulz's children dragged blankets around, so Schulz decided to make it part of the strip.

On November 30, 1954, another new character appeared. Her name was Charlotte Braun, an obvious takeoff on the name Charlie Brown. She even called herself Good Ol' Charlotte Braun. Her main trait was speaking in a loud, thundering voice. Schulz conveyed this by printing the words in her dialogue bubbles in huge capital letters.

In one strip Charlie Brown says that Charlotte is

powered by a "built-in hi-fidelity speaker."[10] Charlotte Braun defends herself by saying she is just a person with a "driving personality [and] definite opinions."[11]

Charlotte Braun was in the strip for just a little more than two months, with her final appearance on February 1, 1955. Some *Peanuts* historians feel her personality was too close to Lucy's for her to serve a purpose in the strip. She was the first failed character in *Peanuts*.

It was now obvious that *Peanuts* was no ordinary comic strip. For one thing, there was a realism among its characters, something rarely seen before on the comics page. Schulz explained, "The initial theme of *Peanuts* was based on the cruelty that exists among children. I recall all too vividly the struggle that takes place out on the playground. This is a struggle that adults grow away from and seem to forget about."[12]

Apparently other cartoonists also remembered the childhood insults and understood the humor Schulz used to deal with them. In 1955 he won the Reuben Award, given annually by the National Cartoonists Society to the best cartoonist of the year. It is the highest award a cartoonist can win.

Flying Kites and Selling Cars

In 1956, comic strip readers encountered something they had never seen before— a verbal running gag. In a strip that ran on April 12, Charlie Brown gets his kite stuck in a tree. As he stands still, holding the kite string, Violet asks what he is going to do. Charlie Brown says, "Nothing . . . I'm so mad I'm just going to stand here for the rest of my life!"[1]

For the next seven days, the *Peanuts* strip jokes centered on the same scene: Charlie Brown standing under the tree, gripping the string, refusing to move. In the finale, it starts to rain. Charlie Brown is getting soaked and is told to come indoors. Is the kite getting wet as well? he wonders. Learning that the kite too is drenched, Charlie Brown smiles and drops the string.

Now that he knows the kite is suffering, he feels ready to walk away.

Other cartoonists had drawn ongoing stories. But there had never been a sequence like this, in which the main characters do nothing but talk for so long a time. This was a turning point in *Peanuts* and added to the comic strip's uniqueness. Readers questioned the meaning behind Charlie Brown's lack of action. One member of the clergy used it as the basis for a sermon on dedication. Schulz said it was a matter of patience and how a person should allow enough time to see how problems can work out.[2]

By 1956, *Peanuts* was being published in more than one hundred newspapers.[3] Additional running gags were introduced: Linus would go into fits when it was time for his blanket to be washed. Charlie Brown found more and more creative ways to lose baseball games. "Good Grief!" and "Rats!" became two of Charlie Brown's favorite expressions—and household words across the United States. Snoopy behaved more and more like a person. He danced on two legs to show how happy he was, which constantly frustrated Lucy. The inside of Snoopy's doghouse was never shown, but the kids often crawled inside and chatted about how spacious it was. It was even said to have a recreation room in its basement. Then, on December 16, 1956, Lucy pulled a football away just as Charlie Brown tried to kick it. That would become an ongoing torment for poor Charlie Brown.

Snoopy had become such a major player that Holt, Rinehart and Winston decided he merited his own book. The fifth *Peanuts* collection, called *Snoopy,*

Will Charlie Brown ever be able to trust Lucy?

came out in 1958. Every strip between the covers of the book features the lovable beagle. It was also in 1958 that Snoopy first walked regularly on his hind legs. Schulz said that opened up a whole new range of potential adventures for Charlie Brown's dog. At home in the Schulz family, a new range of adventures was taking place too, with the birth of their fifth child, a daughter they named Jill.

Peanuts was unique among comic strips in another way. The kids talked about their teachers and parents, but except for a few experimental early strips, the grown-ups were not shown. In a few of the early comic strips, an adult sometimes spoke from outside the scene. In one, Linus's mother scolds him for bothering Lucy and tells him to behave. The dialogue bubble arrow points beyond the frame. Yet even that small adult presence was soon phased out.

On the newsstands, fans could still purchase comic book collections of the antics of Charlie Brown and the gang. All these strips had first appeared in newspapers. Then, in the late 1950s, this changed; new comic books were produced with brand-new stories—and they were not all created by Charles Schulz. Although Schulz had always prided himself on drawing every line in the strip for newspaper publication, he made an exception for the comic books.

The *Peanuts* comic book stories were written and drawn by other artists. The majority were created by Dale Hale, a former employee of Art Instruction Schools. Although Hale was about ten years younger than Schulz, the two cartoonists became good friends. While Hale created and drew the *Peanuts* comic book stories, he stressed, "Sparky didn't give up control. He approved and disapproved them before they went into print."[4]

"The comic books were slightly different than the strips in that they had more action," said Hale. "There were things like little cars zipping by and more kids throwing balls and things."[5] Some situations were highly unusual for the world of Charlie Brown. In one comic strip story, called "Mechanical Maniac," a robot runs wild through the neighborhood. Such fantastic comic book situations never found their way into Schulz's daily strip.

It was not just kids who loved reading *Peanuts*;

adults too were becoming devoted to Charlie Brown and his friends. A 1958 article in *Time* magazine reported that among the regular *Peanuts* readers were the respected poet Carl Sandburg and the president of General Motors, Harlow Curtice.[6]

That was just the way Schulz intended it. His son Craig later said, "My dad never saw himself as writing towards kids. The strip was more geared towards adults."[7]

What was it in *Peanuts* that drew adults like few other comic strips that featured children? For one thing, much of the humor was very subtle. That was a departure from heavy-handed, one-line gags and slapstick humor found in other popular comics of the day. For example, in one 1958 strip Charlie Brown tells Violet how much he admires Linus. "He's read *Cinderella, Pinocchio, Snow White* . . . all of those books. And that isn't the ONLY thing," he adds. "He can also discuss them intelligently."[8] Adult readers can find humor in that sly put-down of people who like to brag about what they have read but cannot talk about the books themselves.

In some ways the *Peanuts* children were like mini-adults. Real seven- or eight-year-old children did not worry about the meaning of life the way Charlie Brown did; nor did they talk about great literature like Linus. Having these comments come out of children's mouths, instead of adults', made them profound—and funny.

Finally, many readers saw *Peanuts* as a satire about society. Child psychology was a growing field in the late 1950s. That is when Schulz first drew Lucy sitting at a little booth, selling "psychiatric help" for five cents. To social critics, Schulz was mocking the so-called experts giving out opinions on child psychology. And while the experts charge high fees for their advice, Schulz seemed to be saying it was really worth about five cents.

Publicly, Schulz never claimed to be making statements about such adult topics as child psychology. He said he created Lucy's psychiatric-help stand simply because he thought it would be funny. "The booth really was a take-off on the lemonade stands that appeared for years in other kid strips," he said.[9]

Was Schulz just being modest? Craig Schulz believes his father's public comments were basically true. "Most of his strips could be seen as being multi-level," noted Craig, "but most of what he drew in the beginning were just things he thought were funny. A lot of people found something on a higher level. Religious groups did a lot of overanalyzing. Often, it was simply a funny idea."[10]

Schulz's cartoonist friend Cathy Guisewite, who draws the comic strip *Cathy*, stated that Schulz's attitude underscored how creative he was. She said, "When people saw all sorts of meanings in his work, he would always kind of roll his eyes and say he was just trying to make his deadline. But I saw him as writing from the heart and soul. He created something millions of people could respond to in different ways. The whole spectrum of humanity could see something different in what he wrote. He depicted what were pure moments to him."[11]

The popularity of *Peanuts* was skyrocketing. In 1958

Many readers viewed Peanuts *as a satire about society. But Schulz often responded that he simply drew "funny comic strips for the newspapers."*

it was being published in more than four hundred newspapers.[12] In the world of business, ideas started spinning. Was the time ripe to sell *Peanuts* beyond the daily and Sunday newspaper comics? One company thought that people would buy dolls in the likenesses of the *Peanuts* characters. This type of business is called *merchandising*.

Still, nobody could use Schulz's characters without his permission. That would be stealing. Schulz created the *Peanuts* characters, and he had the legal right to control their use. It was only fair that he receive a portion of the money made from selling their images. In addition, Schulz did not want to see his characters used in ways he considered degrading or in poor taste.

The legal term for giving others permission to use one's creations is *licensing*. In 1958 the first *Peanuts* characters were licensed, and fans could buy plastic dolls of Charlie Brown and Snoopy. Meanwhile, as the toys were being stocked in stores across the country, Schulz's work earned him another notable honor. Yale University, in New Haven, Connecticut, one of the nation's top colleges, named him Humorist of the Year.

Schulz spent much time that year packing up his paper, drawing board, and other household possessions. The Schulzes were on the move again, this time to the town of Sebastopol, California, about sixty miles north of San Francisco. Schulz said the trip west was his wife's idea. "Joyce was a restless person," he said. "She was fed up with living in the snows of Minnesota, putting the kids in snowsuits every time they went outside. . . . We'd never heard of

Sebastopol, but as soon as we went up the driveway we knew it was the place. . . . It looked like northern Minnesota."[13]

The sprawling home had belonged to a photographer named Rolla Watts. Because it was located on Coffee Lane, Watts had named his house Coffee Grounds. The Schulzes kept the name, displaying it on a sign outside their home.

Schulz's family was complete, but Charlie Brown's was still growing. His sister, Sally, was born on

Lucy the dog joined the Schulz family for a portrait. From left: Dorothy Halverson (Joyce's mother), Craig, Meredith, Monte, Charles, Amy, Joyce, and Jill.

May 25, 1959. In the strip, Charlie Brown is told on the telephone that he is a brother. He runs out of the house screaming with glee, "I'm a father! I mean my dad's a father! I'm a brother! I have a baby sister!! I'm a brother!" In the last frame of the strip, Linus turns to Lucy and says, "You didn't act like that when I was born!"[14]

On October 26, 1959, a classic *Peanuts* running gag was introduced. Linus speaks with awe of the Great Pumpkin, whom he confuses with Santa Claus. He tells Lucy, "I can see him now rising up out of the pumpkin patch with his bag of toys!"[15] In the *Peanuts* strip published on October 29, Linus explains to Charlie Brown, "And then on Halloween night the 'Great Pumpkin' rises up out of the pumpkin patch . . . and brings toys to all the good little children in the world!" Charlie Brown responds, "You're crazy!" And Linus answers, "All right, so you believe in Santa Claus and I'll believe in the 'Great Pumpkin.' The way I see it, it doesn't matter what you believe just so you're sincere."[16]

Some people interpreted Linus's punch line as a

PEANUTS reprinted by permission of United Feature Syndicate, Inc.

Every Halloween, Linus looks forward to toys from the Great Pumpkin.

comment about the many religions in the world. Perhaps Schulz was saying there are many paths to God. Typically, Schulz downplayed such talk. It was simply a comment on how Christmas had become so commercialized, he said.

With *Peanuts* a huge success, it was natural that businesses would want to enlist Schulz's characters to sell their products. Marketing executives believed that the round-headed kid, the fanciful beagle, the boy with the blanket, and the crabby girl would draw people's attention to their products.

José Cuauhtemoc ("Bill") Melendez was a masterful animator in Los Angeles who had worked on several Walt Disney classics, including *Fantasia*, *Pinocchio*, and *Bambi*. In the mid-1950s he was employed by a well-known advertising agency, the J. Walter Thompson Company. A variety of other businesses, including the Ford Motor Company, hired the J. Walter Thompson Company to create their advertisements. Ford was coming out with a new model car called the Falcon. They were searching for a creative way to sell this new car on television. Could the *Peanuts* gang help sell cars?

Melendez said that it was the granddaughter of Norman Strauss, the agency's head, who suggested they use the *Peanuts* characters in their new ad campaign.[17] Strauss himself was not familiar with *Peanuts*, so one of his employees described the comic strip. Strauss said the idea was worth exploring. Other workers at J. Walter Thompson agreed.

As with the plastic dolls, Schulz's permission would be needed to use his characters. Melendez was uneasy about meeting with Schulz.[18] He remembered, "I was told I would have to audition for Schulz since he doesn't like Hollywood or New York animators. And I'm from Hollywood. So we went over to meet Sparky at his home in Sebastopol. I showed him my illustrations [of the *Peanuts* characters]. He wasn't very impressed, but he thought they were okay. We asked him if he would see anything wrong about saying something nice about the Ford Motor Company. Schulz saw no problem. He said, 'All I have ever driven are Fords.'"[19]

The *Peanuts* gang made its television debut in 1959 as cartoon spokespersons for the new car. It was the first time the characters appeared in animated form.

On the newspaper page, Sally Brown was beginning to grow up. She took her first steps on August 22, 1960. The next day she fell in love with Linus; little hearts swirl above her head as she helps him carry his blanket.

She was also portrayed that year as a child who had difficulty learning. Charlie Brown becomes frustrated with her when she has trouble counting. So he shows her a picture with boats in it and asks her to tell him how many boats she sees. "All of them," says Sally.[20]

The trend to license the gang was growing. Hallmark Cards, Inc., released greeting cards featuring *Peanuts* characters in 1960. Charlie Brown, Snoopy, and the rest delivered birthday greetings and get-well wishes. The foundation of a cartoon empire was being built. It would only get bigger.

Charlie Brown: Television Star

Where did Charles Schulz get his ideas? It is harder than one might think to sit every day in front of a blank piece of paper that needs to be filled with a cleverly drawn comic strip. One of Schulz's friends was cartoonist Lynn Johnston, creator of *For Better or For Worse*. She said it was especially hard for Schulz because he never used ideas that were not his own.

Schulz liked to say that he did not know where he got ideas.[1] Many just came to him. Watching a leaf fall outside his studio window could trigger an idea. He could come up with a gag by watching his children, as happened with his daughter Meredith and her toy piano. Often he drew on an incident or feeling from his own childhood. "All of my fears, my anxieties, my joys, and almost even all of my experiences go into that strip," he said.[2] In one strip Charlie Brown waits in line at a movie theater just to get a free candy bar. Just like Charles Schulz when he was a child, Charlie Brown misses out on getting his candy bar by being one person too late.

On occasion it took a friend to push Schulz in the right direction. Lynn Johnston remembered, "One time he called me and said he was depressed because he could not think of a daily strip. He said he was on the bungee cord of life. I told him that was a daily [strip] right there. He didn't use it then, but some time later he called me and I told him to use it. I had to repeat word by word the conversation to convince him that he came up with the line, not me."[3]

Sometimes Schulz's former coworkers set off his imagination. On March 6, 1961, he introduced Frieda, a girl most proud of what she called her naturally curly hair. In one strip Charlie Brown tells Frieda that she will play center field on the baseball team. Her response is, "From that distance do you think people will be able to tell that I have naturally curly hair?"[4] The character Frieda was inspired by Schulz's coworker Frieda Rich from his days at Art Instruction Schools, Inc. "I suppose I introduced her to pep up the strip," said Schulz.[5]

He pepped up the strip even more that year when Frieda announced she was getting a cat. Frieda explains that Snoopy is too smug because he is the only animal in the neighborhood. "Somebody has to put him in his place!" she declares.[6] Frieda names her cat Faron, after country music singer Faron Young.

Where did Schulz get his ideas? Anything could trigger a comic strip.

When she shows Faron to Snoopy, Snoopy thinks, "To me, cats are the crab grass in the lawn of life!"[7]

Faron made a few more appearances in *Peanuts*, but that was all. Schulz's daughter Amy Johnson noted, "Dad hates cats and never liked drawing the cat, and there was never enough for Frieda and the cat to do."[8] He also said that the cat was making Snoopy act more like a regular dog and not like the unique animal he had become. Like Good Ol' Charlotte Braun, Faron was one of *Peanuts'* few failed characters.

Schulz introduced another character in 1961, but an unusual one. She was never seen—at least not in the comic strip. She was only talked about. It was the little red-haired girl. Schulz said he would never draw her. He believed her character would be strongest if readers pictured her in their imaginations.

Charlie Brown had a crush on her but could admire her only from afar. Like Charles Schulz and the pretty girl on the train years earlier, Charlie Brown did not know what to say to the little red-haired girl. He sat on a bench at school eating lunch by himself, wishing he had the courage to talk to her. In one strip Charlie Brown says to himself, "I wonder what would happen if I walked over, and asked her to eat lunch with me. She'd probably laugh in my face. It's hard on a face when it gets laughed in."[9] Schulz later admitted that the little red-haired girl was based on Donna Mae Johnson, the woman who had turned him down to marry another man.

By then Schulz and his family were living very well at their home in Sebastopol. They had three cars, a

*Charlie Brown has a hopeless crush on the little red-haired girl—
and his friends and family love to tease him.*

private tennis court, a swimming pool, formal gardens, and a slew of pets. Included were five dogs, horses, a rabbit, and—even though cats were not his favorite animals—a calico cat. His daughter Amy Johnson said, "We hardly ever took a vacation. We just stayed home at our little Disneyland, as I called it."[10]

Much of the mail Schulz received at his studio was full of compliments. Fans loved writing to tell Schulz about their favorite characters or a recent strip that had made them laugh. He received a share of angry letters also. Schulz was the first major cartoonist to have his characters quote the Bible, and he heard from readers who thought that practice was sacrilegious.

One suggestion he received in the mail was from a San Francisco woman named Connie Boucher. She thought a *Peanuts* date book was a great idea and that it would sell very well. Of course, she needed Schulz's permission to go ahead with such a project.

It sounded wonderful to Schulz. The date book was published soon afterward under the name of

Boucher's business, Determined Productions. Boucher then came up with an idea for a different kind of *Peanuts* book. Instead of a collection of comic strips, this would include about thirty original cartoons that Schulz would draw and write. Each one-panel cartoon would illustrate random thoughts about what happiness is to a child. The title was taken from a *Peanuts* strip in which Lucy hugs Snoopy tightly and says, "Happiness is a warm puppy."

Unlike the *Peanuts* collection books, this book would have a hard cover. It would be more expensive than a paperback, and that was a bit of a risk. Would people be willing to pay more for this book?

Happiness Is a Warm Puppy was published in December 1962. Schulz said the book was about the "little moments you remember when you stop and think back over your life. The happy times were not the artificial delights you paid a lot for but the simple things—like getting together with a few friends."[11]

In one drawing, Snoopy sits atop his doghouse with two birds on each side of him. "Happiness is getting together with your friends," reads the caption. A cartoon of Violet roller-skating says, "Happiness is a smooth sidewalk."[12]

The publication of *Happiness Is a Warm Puppy* was not the only highlight for Schulz at the end of 1962. He earned another honor when the National Cartoonists Society named *Peanuts* the Best Comic Strip of the Year. Meanwhile, Connie Boucher's and Schulz's risk paid off. *Happiness Is a Warm Puppy* was number one on *The New York Times* list of best-selling books for forty-five weeks from late 1962

With licensing, Peanuts fans could buy dolls and stuffed animals of their favorite characters.

through most of 1963. It was followed in 1963 by a similar book, also published by Determined Productions, called *Security Is a Thumb and a Blanket*. Over the next eight years, a total of ten such books would be written by Schulz and published by Determined Productions.

While *Happiness Is a Warm Puppy* highlighted the gentle side of *Peanuts*, Schulz was hardly finished with his biting comments about society. In the early 1960s, credit cards were becoming commonplace, and the ZIP code was instituted by the United States Postal Service. Social Security numbers had already been around for thirty years. Many people were overwhelmed by all these numbers. Some joked that in the future human beings would be known by numbers instead of names.

Schulz took that concern to heart. In 1963 he created a new character: a boy wearing a white T-shirt and short-cropped hair. His name is 5. He has two sisters, named 4 and 3. He explains to Linus, "My dad says we have so many numbers these days we're all losing our identity. He decided that everyone in our family should have a number instead of a name."[13]

When he explains his father's logic to Lucy, she responds, "This is his way of protesting, huh?" And 5 replies, "No, this is his way of giving in!"[14]

Another person who contacted Schulz to use his characters in a project was a young filmmaker from San Francisco named Lee Mendelson. In 1963 Mendelson had just finished producing a documentary about baseball great Willie Mays. Noting the tremendous popularity of *Happiness Is a Warm*

Puppy, Mendelson thought people might want to know more about the man who created *Peanuts.*

Schulz agreed to work with the young documentary producer. Mendelson got a San Francisco–based jazz pianist and *Peanuts* fan named Vince Guaraldi to play the background music. He then recruited Bill Melendez, the animator who drew the *Peanuts* characters in the Ford television ads, to do the drawings.

The result was a thirty-minute film biography about Schulz. Mendelson hoped to sell it to a television network. "But in true Charlie Brown fashion, no one was interested," Mendelson later wrote.[15]

Some have said Schulz's gift of humor was special in that it could be appreciated by people of all ages and of all backgrounds. This was proved in 1964 when a man studying to be a Methodist minister came out with a different kind of *Peanuts* book. Robert L. Short saw the characters in *Peanuts*— Charlie Brown always losing baseball games, Linus clinging to his security blanket, and the rest of the gang—as symbols of people in the Bible. So he wrote a book called *The Gospel According to Peanuts,* offering biblical interpretations of the comic strip.

Although Schulz had given Short permission to use his characters, Schulz had nothing to do with the writing and sale of the book. He publicly disagreed with several of Short's conclusions, but he and Short got to know each other and became very good friends. *The Gospel According to Peanuts* became a best-seller.

The *Peanuts* comic books created by other cartoonists were phased out around this time, but the paperback collections of Schulz's newspaper strips were as popular as ever. So were the little hardcover books published by Determined Productions. And the honors kept coming. Schulz won a second Reuben Award in 1964.

Although Lee Mendelson's film about Schulz never made it to television, some insiders in the advertising business saw it and liked it. One was John Allen, who worked for the advertising agency McCann-Erickson. Allen called Mendelson in April 1965, and their conversation made television history.

Allen asked Mendelson if he and Schulz had ever considered doing a Christmas special. Mendelson later wrote: "'Of course' I replied, not bothering to think about what I was saying."[16] Allen explained that one of his clients, Coca-Cola, wanted to sponsor a television special around the holidays but did not have a program to work with.

Mendelson met with Schulz and the two zipped into action. They recruited Bill Melendez and Vince Guaraldi to do the animation and music. Schulz insisted that the special had to deal with the true meaning of Christmas. He also wanted it to include winter scenes typical of his childhood in Minnesota, with lots of snow and ice-skating.

Mendelson and Melendez worked together on the storyboard—a rough drawing plotting the scenes of the feature cartoon. Schulz liked their work but asked for one addition to the story line. He wanted Linus to quote the biblical book of Luke, chapter 2, verses 8 through 14, which tells much of the Christmas story. Melendez said, "I told him I thought it was a bad idea to quote the Bible in a cartoon. He looked at me coldly with his beady blue eyes and said, 'If we don't do it, who will?'"[17]

At first, the network that would air the show, CBS-TV, wanted an hour-long special. Melendez said while that would be fine for a movie, it was too long for an animated television show. He persuaded the network to cut the time to thirty minutes.

By the time business matters were settled, there were just four months left until the program was to air. The crew rushed to meet the deadline. Melendez confessed, "When I finished the show, I said, 'We killed it.' All the other people in my office said it was great. But the drawings were dreadful. We cheapened it, trying to do it cheap within a tight budget. I didn't stay within the budget, seventy-five thousand dollars for the half hour show. It cost me ninety-six thousand dollars to do it."[18]

A Charlie Brown Christmas aired on December 9, 1965. Melendez was not the only person to dislike it. Schulz's son Monte declared, "I was horrified at the way the kids spoke and to see the animation. It was not as good as Dad's drawing, and the execution was a huge disappointment."[19]

Most television watchers felt just the opposite. *A Charlie Brown Christmas* was seen in more than 15 million homes across the United States on that Thursday evening, making it the second most watched television program that week.[20] Only *Bonanza*, a popular western series, had more viewers. *A Charlie Brown Christmas* was honored with an Emmy Award, given by the television industry only to programs it considers the absolute best.

In spite of that fantastic showing, Bill Melendez still says, "I always wince when I watch the show because I'm embarrassed by it. But our fans like it and think it's wonderful. As soon as I drew it I wanted to get rid of the drawings [now known as cel art]. I called the [United Feature] syndicate and they didn't want them. I called Sparky and he didn't want them. So I threw them out. When people today hear I threw away the drawings, they almost faint."[21]

The New Neighborhood

Was Charlie Brown really Charles Schulz? In other words, did the cartoonist base his main character on his own childhood? Some observers said yes, but Schulz always claimed there was a little bit of him in all his characters.

In 1965 a purely Charlie Brown–type of incident happened to the cartoonist. Schulz, by then a household name, had grown into a tall, handsome man with a distinguished appearance. Some of his high school classmates were compiling names of their fellow graduates for an upcoming reunion. Schulz's name was on the list of "missing" people. They did not know what had happened to him. They did not imagine the famous Charles Schulz was the same awkward and pimply-faced kid they had grown up with.

Was Charlie Brown really Charles Schulz? The cartoonist said he put some of himself into all his characters.

One day at home, Schulz glanced at a candy dish and noticed a mint chocolate called a Peppermint Patty. What a great name for a cartoon character, he thought.[1] "So in this case I created the character to fit the name," he said.[2]

A cute name was not the only reason Peppermint Patty joined *Peanuts*. "I wanted to develop someone from another neighborhood who could challenge Charlie Brown's team, and perhaps challenge Lucy, too," said Schulz. "I also believe that a comic artist and a comic strip have to grow. If you just stand still and play off past successes, you're liable to fail in the long run."[3]

Peppermint Patty first appeared on August 22, 1966. In a strip that ran shortly afterward, she offered to help Charlie Brown's baseball team. Peppermint Patty pitched superbly in her first game, but it was not enough. Even though she had pitched a no-hitter and hit five home runs herself, the team was still losing 37–5. "Whoever heard of thirty-seven unearned runs? This is ridiculous!" she screams.[4]

The *Peanuts* gang played ball on television, too. After the success of *A Charlie Brown Christmas*, more animated *Peanuts* specials were planned. One about baseball, *Charlie Brown's All-Stars*, aired in the summer of 1966. A third show, *It's the Great Pumpkin, Charlie Brown*, was screened that fall. *Peanuts* animator Bill Melendez has said that the Halloween special is his all-time favorite.[5]

To Schulz there was a big difference between the television cartoon specials and the comic strip. Craig Schulz said that unlike his father's comic strip, the television shows were geared mainly toward children.

Sometimes the *Peanuts* characters showed up in the most unlikely places. In the mid-1960s, Schulz's son Monte had a hobby building plastic World War I model airplanes. Before long, Snoopy was play-acting as a World War I flying ace. He would sit atop his doghouse, which he pretended was a Sopwith Camel fighter plane. Snoopy imagined himself flying over France trying to bring down the German flying ace known as the Red Baron. This series of cartoons was hugely popular.

One day in late 1966, a friend complimented Schulz on his song being played on the radio. What song was that? Schulz wondered. He learned that a rock group from Florida, the Royal Guardsmen, had a hit novelty record called "Snoopy vs. the Red Baron." For four weeks in December 1966 and January 1967, it was the number-two song in the nation.[6] A song by the red-hot group the Monkees kept it from reaching number one.

The trouble was that neither the Royal Guardsmen nor anyone involved in producing the record had asked Schulz's permission to use the *Peanuts* characters' names in the song. Schulz's attorney contacted the record company, and as a result of their discussions Schulz began to receive a percentage of the royalty payments the record earned.

Craig Schulz, who was thirteen at the time, said the rock group did not mean any harm to his father. "They were probably just a bunch of kids who hammered out a record," he concluded. "They probably didn't even know there was a copyright."[7]

Craig said that his father liked the song, which was obviously intended as a tribute. In fact, the Royal Guardsmen released several follow-up Snoopy songs. The most successful of these was "The Return of the Red Baron," which peaked at number fifteen on the charts in the spring of 1967. Also that spring, another rock group jumped on the Snoopy bandwagon. The Sopwith Camel, a quartet of young men from San Francisco, had a top-thirty hit called "Hello Hello."[8]

Craig Schulz explained that it was important for his father to make sure he received royalties from the sales of the Royal Guardsmen's Snoopy songs. "A lot of people don't even know about things like copyrights and royalties," he said, "but you have to protect your property or it won't be yours."[9]

One person well aware of copyrights was a New York–based songwriter named Clark Gesner. Gesner was working as a composer for the popular children's television program *Captain Kangaroo* when he decided to try his hand at writing songs about the *Peanuts* kids, with singers portraying the various characters. Gesner thought that they would make a fine record.

Gesner sent Schulz a demo record—a recording made solely to demonstrate what the songs sounded like. Then he had to wait for a reply. "I was awakened from a nap by Mr. Schulz calling me and saying these were fine. He was very honored that I put so much care into the songs," recalled Gesner.[10]

After the record was made, the woman who sang as Lucy played it for a theater producer named Arthur Whitelaw. He loved it and thought the songs would make the basis for a wonderful musical play. Gesner was not so sure. "I thought that to try to put it on stage would be a violation of what people knew the characters looked like," he said. "I just thought it would make a great record. It would become a virtual play just by people listening to it."[11]

Whitelaw persuaded Gesner to give it a try. Gesner got busy writing dialogue for the characters. He admitted that the dialogue was basically "lifting quotes from the strip."[12] Gesner completed the play, and the main characters were cast. Whitelaw and coproducer Gene Person presented *You're a Good Man, Charlie Brown* for the first time in a theater in the East Village section of New York City on March 7, 1967. The next day Walter Kerr of *The New York Times* gave it a glowing review. *You're a Good Man, Charlie Brown* was a sensation.

Schulz's cartoon had become the foundation of a major commercial empire. In addition to books, Determined Productions was also marketing *Peanuts* stuffed animals and other products. Plush Snoopys were as popular as teddy bears on children's wish lists.

In the wake of Peppermint Patty's first appearance, Schulz introduced other characters from her neighborhood. In March 1967 Peppermint Patty brings a boy of mixed heritage to play on Charlie Brown's hapless baseball team. His name is José Peterson. Peppermint Patty says that with her pitching and José Peterson's skill at second base, the team will be great. After a week, though, José Peterson gives up, just as Peppermint Patty had done earlier. Peppermint Patty tells Charlie Brown that she and

José have decided to start their own team in their neighborhood.

"Frankly, I don't think your team is ever going to amount to much," she informs him. "Chuck, you just don't have it. Maybe you could try shuffleboard or something like that. Well, we've got a long way to go so we'd better say good-bye. José Peterson's mom is having me over tonight for tortillas and Swedish meatballs!"[13]

The next year an African-American child named Franklin joined the strip. Franklin and Charlie Brown meet at the beach, and later Franklin appears sitting at the desk in front of Peppermint Patty at school. Charles Schulz was one of the first cartoonists to include an African-American character in a major comic strip. It was such a bold step in 1968 that *Newsweek* magazine ran an article about Franklin's debut.

Regular *Peanuts* readers knew that Peppermint Patty lived in a single-parent home with her father. Her neighborhood was tougher, and most likely poorer, than Charlie Brown's neighborhood. In the late 1960s the civil rights movement was in full swing and more attention was being paid to city neighborhoods. In his own way, Schulz was keeping up with the times.

Although Schulz enjoyed living in northern California, there was one thing he missed about Minnesota: ice-skating. An ice arena in the nearby town of Santa Rosa had closed in the late sixties. Schulz's wife, Joyce, suggested the family build an arena for local people to enjoy. Their new ice arena opened in May 1969. The cost was $2 million.[14]

Lacking a place to ice-skate, Schulz built an arena for the residents of his community in California.

That spring was an exciting time. From May 18 through May 26, the *Apollo X* lunar expedition blasted into outer space. This was the last experimental flight before the first moon landing. The astronauts— Eugene A. Cernan, Thomas P. Stafford, and John W. Young—nicknamed their command module "Charlie Brown" and the lunar module "Snoopy." Schulz called the flight "one of the most moving experiences of my entire life."[15] In a speech he said it was amazing how Snoopy had gone from flying a Sopwith Camel to piloting a spacecraft. When the command and lunar modules successfully docked, one of the astronauts announced to mission control, "Snoopy and Charlie Brown are hugging each other."[16]

By the late 1960s, the *Peanuts* characters had triumphed in daily newspapers, books, television, and theater. There was one important medium still to be conquered: movies. That changed in December 1969 when *A Boy Named Charlie Brown*, a full-length movie, opened at Radio City Music Hall in New York City. This eighty-five-minute film boasted the largest advance sale of any movie Radio City had ever shown until that time.[17]

Bill Melendez animated the movie, as he had the television specials. The plot was based on a story from one of the comic strips. Charlie Brown enters a spelling bee and has a chance to win. Typically, he blows it at the end. When asked to spell the word *maze*, Charlie Brown's first thought is baseball player Willie Mays. So that is how he spells the word: *M-A-Y-S*. Linus consoles him, assuring Charlie Brown that the world has not come to an end just because he did not win. Three more *Peanuts* feature movies would be made over the next several years.

A *Charlie Brown Christmas* ran on television for the fifth time in December 1969, with an audience of roughly 55 million people. That same night *A Boy Named Charlie Brown* opened to a capacity crowd at Radio City Music Hall. *You're a Good Man, Charlie Brown* was still packing the house in a New York theater, and more than 100 million people read *Peanuts* in the daily newspapers.[18] Charles Schulz had conquered all media. *Peanuts* was a true American institution.

"What Do You Think Security Is?"

To those who knew Charles Schulz only as a name in the papers, the cartoonist and his family seemed to be leading a charmed life. They lived on a rambling estate, Schulz earned more money in a year than many people earned in a lifetime, and he had a creative job that brought him fans all over the world.

Yet all was not as it seemed.

Schulz had earned a reputation in northern California as a very private person. He claimed that that was not really true. "Oh, we go to San Francisco about once a month, see friends, go to a play," he said. "But we aren't nightclubbers or cocktail types. Neither of us drink, never have, just isn't part of our life and our friends just have to accept us like that."[1]

It was true that Schulz preferred to stay close to home. Traveling could be stressful, though his children have different views on how much it bothered him. Son Craig said his father would get nervous preparing to go away, but could relax once he was on the actual trip. Daughter Amy believes her father was rarely comfortable in strange places. She remembered, "One reason was that he had a weak stomach and had a fear he would get a stomachache while away from home. He would buy luggage for a trip and plan and prepare for the trip and then not get on the plane. Obviously he did have some anxiety if he got to the point of canceling trips."[2]

"One time he was supposed to go to London for Wimbledon, I think," said Amy. "Then we got a call that he didn't get on the plane. So my brother and I went over to the house and he was sitting by himself watching TV. I said, 'You have to go to London.' He said, 'I don't have to do anything I don't want to.'"[3]

Schulz agreed to fly to London that day, as long as someone went with him. Monte went along on the trip. "He could have gotten many honors but only if he would travel to get them, and he wouldn't travel," said Amy.[4]

Like other artists in similar situations, Schulz found benefits to his depression, sadness, and fears. Craig Schulz explained, "He took his depression and used it as a tool. He tried not to let it control his life, but if it wasn't for the depression, he wouldn't have drawn the cartoon for fifty years and gotten some of the ideas he did."[5]

One classic example is a Sunday comic strip in

which Charlie Brown and Peppermint Patty are sitting beneath a tree. Peppermint Patty asks, "What do you think security is, Chuck?" He replies that security is being a little kid and sleeping in the backseat of the family car. You don't have to worry about anything, since your parents are in control. Peppermint Patty smiles.

Then Charlie Brown adds: "But it doesn't last! Suddenly, you're grown up, and it can never be that way again. Suddenly, it's over, and you'll never get to sit in the back seat again! Never!"

"Never?" worries Peppermint Patty, to which Charlie Brown responds, "Absolutely never!"

"Hold my hand, Chuck!!" begs Peppermint Patty. "Hold my hand, Chuck!!"[6]

Peanuts fans did not know that the Schulzes' marriage was in trouble. According to their son Monte, "They just were growing apart. They had different ambitions."[7]

Despite the personal problems in his life, Schulz continued working hard at his job, and *Peanuts* continued to evolve. In 1970 one of Snoopy's bird friends was given the name Woodstock and became part of the regular *Peanuts* cast. Snoopy had been interacting with various birds for years, but one clumsy and lightheaded fellow seemed to be his favorite. Schulz named him after the landmark rock concert that had taken place just a year earlier near Woodstock, New York.

A language fad inspired one of Snoopy's personalities. Craig Schulz and his friends were using *Joe* as a catchall name for people and their personalities: For

Schulz used the ups and downs of his life as a tool in creating his comic strips.

example, someone popular and in control of situations was dubbed "Joe Cool." Schulz borrowed the nickname from Craig and his buddies, portraying Snoopy as a calm and collected college student who wore a sweater and sunglasses and went by the name Joe Cool.

Schulz's daughter Amy was in high school at the time. Like her father, she was a poor student. "School was very hard," she said later. "I never understood anything. I don't know how I made it out of high school. I hated it with a passion."[8]

Schulz transferred such frustration to Peppermint Patty and Sally Brown. Peppermint Patty often fell asleep at her desk and rarely received a grade other than a D-minus. Sally never got the hang of anything, including arithmetic. In one strip Sally says, "Two times two is tooty-two. Three times three is threety-three and four times four is four-forty-four!" She then tells her brother, "I thought I was going to have trouble with multiplication, but I don't find it hard at all."[9]

Amy Johnson explained, "Peppermint Patty and Sally probably reflect what [my father] went through and probably what most people go through, except those who are so smart that everybody hates them because it's so easy for them."[10]

Peanuts was more than twenty years old and had more fans than ever. Meanwhile another comic strip was moving into center field. Where the media once embraced *Peanuts* for its daring and originality, some writers were now finding fault with the strip. *Doonesbury*, drawn by Garry Trudeau, was the new favorite of the critics. Through his characters Mike Doonesbury, Zonker Harris, Joanie Caucus, and Mark Slackmeyer, Trudeau made biting comments on political issues. One of his favorite targets was the controversial Vietnam War. Some readers began to regard *Peanuts* as lightweight compared to the more heavy-hitting *Doonesbury*.

It is true that *Peanuts* characters never made the kind of stinging remarks found in *Doonesbury*. But critics were wrong when they said Schulz completely shied away from political or social commentary. His character 5 is a perfect example. Another is Miss Tenure, one of the *Peanuts* kids' teachers. *Tenure* is a policy that allows public-school teachers—once they have met certain requirements—to keep their jobs for life. Many people who are not teachers condemn tenure, saying it makes it impossible to fire teachers who do not continue to measure up.

As for politics, Schulz did comment in *Peanuts* on the Vietnam War. When Franklin was introduced, his father was a serviceman fighting in the war. In a series of strips that ran for several days in 1970, Snoopy is invited to give an Independence Day speech to the dogs at his birthplace, the Daisy Hill Puppy Farm. When he steps up to the podium, a riot breaks out. In one cartoon panel, Linus reads the newspaper and reports to Charlie Brown, "According to the paper, the riot was about war dogs. Apparently there's been some trouble about dogs being sent to Viet Nam and then not getting back."[11]

Schulz said that he based the *Peanuts* kids' camp adventures on his experience of being sent away to the army in World War II. It was during a sequence of camp strips in 1971 that Schulz introduced the last major *Peanuts* character. Marcie is a fellow camper with glasses and dark hair who starts calling Peppermint Patty "Sir" in a misguided attempt to be polite. In that first camp series, Peppermint Patty complains about the constant rain while Marcie calmly explains that rain helps farmers.

In school, Marcie sits in the chair behind

Peppermint Patty and often tries to help Peppermint Patty stay awake in class. Even though Marcie is a terrible athlete, Peppermint Patty allows her to play on the neighborhood's various sports teams. For her part, Marcie helps Peppermint Patty complete difficult homework assignments. Although the two girls are very different, they become best friends. The only thing they seem to have in common is that they both like Charlie Brown. Unlike Lucy, the girls in the other neighborhood admire Charlie Brown as a trusting fellow who never gives up.

PEANUTS reprinted by permission of United Feature Syndicate, Inc.

Marcie and Peppermint Patty are best friends.

Meanwhile, the Schulzes' marriage was not getting better. They divorced in 1972. According to Amy Johnson, "I don't think they were really happy except when we were little kids, which is when lots of parents are happy. I know the divorce made him [my father] feel like a failure."[12]

Schulz moved out of his home and into his studio. He slept on the couch and tried to set up housekeeping. Then one day at the ice-skating arena he met Jeannie Forsyth Clyde, an active woman who wrote poetry and had a pilot's license. Soon the two were dating.

In 1972 Lucy and Linus suddenly had a baby brother. In the strip that ran on May 31, Lucy complains, "At first, I wanted to be an only child. You spoiled that! Then I thought maybe it would be kind of nice to have a sister. So what happens? I get another brother. A rerun!"

Linus shouts, "THAT'S IT! We'll call him 'Rerun'!"[13]

And Rerun became the little boy's name.

In 1973, Charles Schulz and Jeannie Forsyth Clyde were married. They settled into a new home in Santa Rosa, California, not far from Schulz's studio and the ice arena.

Success, Failure, and a Desert Rat

Until the mid-1970s readers knew very little about Snoopy's family. Once in a great while he would be drawn thinking about his mother. That was especially true around Mother's Day. Then, in 1975, Schulz's readers discovered that Snoopy had a brother. Schulz named him Spike in honor of the real dog of his childhood who ate weird things such as razor blades.

Spike was first mentioned on August 4, 1975, when it was announced that Snoopy's brother from the desert was coming to visit. Spike resided in Needles, California, the town where Schulz had lived briefly as a boy. A few days later, on August 13, Snoopy calls out, "Eggs Benedict for my brother, Spike!" Lucy responds, "I think you'd better make

Ready . . . action! It's Snoopy on ice! Producer Charles Schulz confers with his big star.

that ten pounds of buffalo steak."[1] In the final frame, the reader sees that Spike is a scrawny dog with a face like Snoopy's, but with a wiry mustache and wearing a cowboy hat. He is the perfect image of a desert rat. A year later, Schulz gave Snoopy and Spike a sister named Belle.

On October 24, 1977, a *Peanuts* television special showed fans something they had never thought they would see. In *It's Your First Kiss, Charlie Brown*, the long-suffering hero escorts the little red-haired girl to the homecoming dance. It is the only time the red-haired girl is ever fully seen in any *Peanuts* project. She even gets a name for the occasion: Heather. Animator Bill Melendez—and not Schulz—was the person to draw her.

How could this be, when Schulz always said he wanted to leave her looks to his readers' imaginations? Monte Schulz said that to his father, the comic strip showed the *real* actions of the *Peanuts* characters. The television programs and movies were just made-up stories using his characters. "The strip was at the heart of Dad's life," said Monte. "Don't associate the shows and the strip together. There is no direct connection between the two."[2]

More honors came to Schulz. In 1978 he was named International Humorist of the Year by the International Pavilion of Humor in Montreal, Quebec, Canada. The next year he served as national chairman of the 1979 Christmas Seals Campaign.

The morning of July 1, 1981, Schulz awoke with a tightness in his chest. At first he thought it was a pain from sleeping crooked.[3] He went to his studio to work, and although the tightness went away, it soon returned. Schulz was suffering a heart attack.

Doctors discovered that four of Schulz's major arteries were clogged. That was slowing down the flow of blood to his heart. In a major surgical procedure called a bypass, doctors rerouted Schulz's blood flow through other, less clogged blood vessels.

Schulz's daughter Jill Schulz Transki was twenty-three years old at the time. She remembered, "Considering the seriousness of it, he was pretty optimistic. But being optimistic on the outside might have just been the way he dealt with it. Inside, he was probably as worried and scared as anyone would be."[4]

About that time, Schulz developed a slight tremble in his hands. It would get worse as time went on, making the lettering of the strip increasingly difficult. That did not stop Schulz, though. He gave Snoopy a new favorite fantasy as a beagle scout, leading Woodstock and his bird friends on nature hikes. Their adventures became a continuing gag.

PEANUTS reprinted by permission of United Feature Syndicate, Inc.

Snoopy the beagle scout takes charge of Woodstock and his little bird friends.

As with Faron the cat in the early 1960s, Schulz freely admitted when he thought he made a mistake. In 1982 Snoopy gained another brother, Marbles. Unlike Spike, who lived in the California desert, Marbles lived near Snoopy. Schulz began to realize that Marbles's personality detracted from Snoopy's. And that was the end of Marbles. Schulz also did away with Snoopy's sister, Belle. He just did not like her, he said.

Longtime readers in the 1980s could not help noticing that some of the earliest characters seemed to have disappeared from the comic strip. These included Shermy, Patty, Violet, Frieda, and 5. After Schulz introduced Peppermint Patty and her friends from the other neighborhood, there did not seem to be much use for the earlier characters. Still, they were never officially written out of the strip.

What happened to them? Of course, the real answer is that they are not real people, so nothing happened to them. But the comic strip world has its own explanations. Monte Schulz said, "I don't know what [my father] ever said happened to these characters. I assume they moved away. It was almost like it was a small neighborhood in the beginning that was growing. As with most neighborhoods, some kids move away. They met and were friends and years later they moved."[5]

A group of fans who maintain a *Peanuts* Web site say these kids are still in the neighborhood but just do not show up in the strip. Characters resembling Patty and Violet have appeared in crowd scenes—at school bus stops, for example. These kids are not identified by name, though, so it is hard to be certain exactly who they are.

Meanwhile, the other characters were getting more visibility. A Saturday morning cartoon series, *The Charlie Brown and Snoopy Show*, premiered in 1983. Episodes included "Linus' Security Blanket," "Peppermint Patty's School Days," and "Lucy Loves Schroeder." The same year, Knott's Berry Farm, a theme park in southern California, opened a section called Camp Snoopy, with *Peanuts*-themed rides and costumed characters.

Also in 1983, a *Peanuts* cartoon special that was particularly meaningful to Schulz debuted on television. *What Have We Learned, Charlie Brown?* featured the *Peanuts* gang observing the Allied invasion of Normandy on the French coast, during World War II. That event, known as D-Day, took place on June 6, 1944, and is viewed by historians as the turning point in the war.

As a World War II veteran, Schulz was a great admirer of General Dwight D. Eisenhower, who was Supreme Commander of the Allied forces during the war. After the program aired, Schulz received letters from young people saying they now better understood the importance of D-Day. The *Peanuts* program won a Peabody Award, which honors excellence in broadcasting.

The next year *Peanuts* reached a notable milestone: It was sold to its two thousandth newspaper.[6] As a result, the *Guinness Book of World Records* listed *Peanuts* as the "world's most popular comic strip."[7]

The Charlie Brown and Snoopy Show aired its final

episode in 1986. Although it ran for three years, the television series was never a critical success. According to Schulz's longtime animator Bill Melendez, "Sparky couldn't work on it—that was what was wrong with it."[8]

In the fall of 1988, an educational *Peanuts* cartoon series was broadcast on television for eight weeks. In each episode of *This Is America, Charlie Brown,* the characters travel back in time to witness a major event in American history. The *Peanuts* gang observe

Every morning Schulz drove to his studio at One Snoopy Place. He often said that he would work at his desk until he wore a hole right through it.

the crossing of the *Mayflower* and the Wright Brothers' first airplane flight, near Kitty Hawk, North Carolina. The *This Is America* series and *The Charlie Brown and Snoopy Show* were rerun years later on the Nickelodeon cable television network.

What was perhaps Schulz's biggest disappointment took place around the same time as these other successes. A *Peanuts* special called *It's the Girl in the Red Truck, Charlie Brown* was televised on September 27, 1988. Schulz had high hopes for this show. He wanted it to be his best ever.[9] Unlike earlier *Peanuts* cartoon specials, this one combined animation and live action. The star was Snoopy's brother Spike, who falls in love with a real live beautiful blonde named Jenny, who drives an old red truck.

This was a very personal show for Schulz for two reasons. Jenny was played by his daughter Jill, and his son Monte wrote the script. Unfortunately, the critics hated it.[10] Some had unkind comments about Jill's acting talent. Bill Melendez thought the script was weak and called it "the worst film we ever did."[11] Jill did not like the directing: "The director told us we have to be happy. We acted sickeningly happy. I cringe at those parts. That's why I don't watch it often. When we acted more real it went all right. Maybe if I did it the way I would have wanted to, with a different director, it would have turned out better."[12]

It's the Girl in the Red Truck, Charlie Brown offered proof that even the best fail now and then.

"You?!"

*P*eanuts entered the 1990s in high gear. What was once viewed as a simple comic strip was now recognized by many experts as legitimate art. A major exhibit of Charles Schulz's work opened at the Louvre in Paris, France. The Louvre is perhaps the world's most famous and most well regarded art museum. Any artist would be thrilled to have an exhibit on the walls of the Louvre.

Charlie Brown and his pals were also celebrated during a halftime show at the 1990 Super Bowl. In 1992, another Camp Snoopy opened up inside the Mall of America, the largest shopping mall in the United States. It is located in Bloomington, Minnesota, outside Schulz's hometown. And more special exhibits of

Schulz's art opened in the major international cities of Rome, Italy; and Montreal, Quebec, Canada.

Schulz's editor at United Media (formerly United Feature Syndicate), Amy Lago, summed up his stature in the world of cartoonists: "He was the king!"[1] Lago was always impressed by Schulz's professionalism. "He was always ahead of deadline, usually three months ahead of schedule with both the Sunday and weekly strips," she said.[2] And he put tremendous care into his work: "The first four years I worked with Sparky he did not have any spelling errors. I couldn't believe the first time we found one. The word was *extension* and he spelled it ending with *t-i-o-n.* I was so surprised to see an error that I had to go to the dictionary to make sure it wasn't an alternative spelling of the word."[3]

One of Schulz's cartoonist friends, Cathy Guisewite, the creator of *Cathy*, said, "I was most impressed by how tidy he was. When I'm done writing, my desk is a total disaster, papers all over the place. His desk was the opposite. It was pristine. He could have taken a lackadaisical attitude, but he never did. Of any cartoonist I have ever met, he worked the hardest."[4]

Meanwhile, on the pages of *Peanuts*, the characters' antics and adventures continued. Linus clutched his security blanket and sucked his thumb. On Halloween, he waited in vain for the Great Pumpkin to appear. Snoopy played his fantasy roles, including Joe Cool, the World War I fighter pilot, and the beagle scout leader. Sally and Peppermint Patty suffered their usual school problems. And Charlie Brown, as

Looking back, looking forward: For Charles Schulz, the year 1990 marked forty years of Peanuts.

hard as he tried, kept missing footballs and striking out in baseball.

Then, on March 30, 1993, the unthinkable happened: Charlie Brown hit a home run.

This was not in the pretend world of *Peanuts* television specials, but in the "real world" of the comic strip. After his home run, Charlie Brown does cartwheels all the way home. His sister Sally is there to greet him at the door. Charlie Brown exclaims, "I hit a home run in the ninth inning, and we won! I was the hero!!" Sally is stunned and utters only one word: "You?!"[5]

It was such a surprise that a television reporter announced Charlie Brown's homer on the *CBS Evening News*. The character who threw the pitch was named Royanne. She said she was the great-granddaughter of Roy Hobbs, the hero of *The Natural*, a baseball novel by Bernard Malamud. *The Natural*, made into a movie in 1984, was very popular, so many people knew the name Roy Hobbs.

Not long afterward in a game against the same team, Charlie Brown hits another home run off Royanne. Again, Charlie Brown beams with pride.

That would soon change. When Royanne meets Charlie Brown for an ice cream sundae, she confesses that she let him hit the home runs. Charlie Brown screams, "You LET me hit those home runs?!" She answers, "I had to Charles. You looked cute standing there at the plate." Charlie Brown, mouth wide open, cries out, *"I didn't want to look cute!!"* In the last frame, Royanne asks, "How about pathetic?" Charlie

Brown leans his head against a tree and mutters, "I can't stand it!"[6]

The next day, Charlie Brown has a surprise for Royanne. He wants to know why she confessed to letting him hit the home runs. "I liked being a hero," he says. She replies, "I'm Roy Hobbs' great-granddaughter. I have a reputation."

When Charlie Brown informs her that "Roy Hobbs was a fictional character," Royanne, baseball cap flying off her head, is shocked. "What?!" she shrieks.

"Didn't you know that?" says Charlie Brown, but Royanne can only sigh, "My life is ruined."[7]

The next day Charlie Brown breaks the news to Linus that he was no hero. "She confessed that she let me hit those home runs! I was crushed! I was humiliated! And then she let me pay for the chocolate sundaes."[8]

No matter how hard he tried, Charlie Brown would never be a real hero. Schulz once declared, "People say, 'Well, why couldn't you have Charlie Brown kick the football.' Well, I could. It would make him happy. And happiness is neat. I wish we could all be happy. But unfortunately, happiness is not very funny."[9]

Still, Schulz always maintained that Charlie Brown was not a loser. A real loser would stop trying. Charlie Brown always had hope.

Although *Peanuts* was carried in more newspapers than ever, the comic strip also had more critics. As they had twenty years earlier when *Doonesbury* first came along, faultfinders said *Peanuts* was behind the times. They said it was not on the cutting edge like *Bloom County*, *Calvin and Hobbes*, and other popular comics of the day. Though they were in the minority, these critics became very vocal, saying that Schulz should let *Peanuts* end.

Schulz had no intention of doing so. Cartoonist Lynn Johnston said, "He'd get furious with writers who were very caustic—who said he should have quit long ago. He said, 'I'm doing the best work I've ever done.'"[10]

Cathy Guisewite added that he could not help taking some of the criticism personally. "I don't know any creative person who is not a fragile ego at heart," she said. "From my experiences with Sparky, he lived in a constant state of self-doubt. He was probably offended by those comments and hurt by them. He probably thought, 'Maybe I'm not any good.'"[11]

Others faulted Schulz for excessive merchandising. They accused him of cheapening his comic strip by allowing images of Charlie Brown, Snoopy, and other *Peanuts* characters to be placed on so many different products. It is true that *Peanuts* had mushroomed into a multimillion-dollar industry. It was estimated that 80 percent of Schulz's income came, not from drawing the comic strip, but from selling the rights to use his characters.[12]

The fact is that Schulz was never overly interested in money. He could have made much greater amounts of money through additional licensing of his characters.[13] He donated millions of dollars to charities including schools, the national memorial to D-Day, and a group called Canine Companions for Independence, which trains dogs to be matched with people who have disabilities other than blindness.

In 1996, the beloved creator of Charlie Brown, Lucy, and Snoopy was honored with a star on the Hollywood Walk of Fame in California.

In addition, Schulz strictly controlled what products would sport the *Peanuts* images. He never allowed Charlie Brown or Linus to appear on anything he thought was in bad taste. Lynn Johnston said, "You should see the stuff he turned down, such as sweaters he didn't like and windup toys that didn't work properly. He rejected three times what he accepted."[14]

Besides, *Peanuts* merchandise served a purpose. Cathy Guisewite believes that merchandising is "a great way to keep the characters alive for people. They become friends for people, like having a *Peanuts* mug on your work desk, having a character who understands you even if no humans do."[15] Lynn Johnston recalled hearing about a fifteen-year-old child who died and was buried with the stuffed Snoopy he loved so much. "That would not have been possible without licensing," she said.[16]

In November 1997 Schulz did something he had never done in his working career: He planned a five-week break in honor of his seventy-fifth birthday. He intended to stay home and relax, doing the things he loved best, such as playing ice hockey and golf. But something funny happened during his third week off. Craig Schulz remembered, "He was pretty much bored to death not working. In the third week he sneaked back into his studio and worked every day. Everyone said he was on vacation so he wouldn't be disturbed. It just showed that his favorite passion was the comic strip."[17]

At the time he began his short vacation, Schulz said, "I have no intention of retiring as long as I feel well. The only thing that would stop me is if I had an illness and couldn't work."[18]

So Charles Schulz kept drawing. To many readers' surprise, on May 25, 1998, the little red-haired girl finally appeared in a daily newspaper strip. Charlie Brown was hoping to dance with her, but he had to wait. She was having too much fun dancing with a different partner—Snoopy. She was visible only in silhouette, so readers could not see her face. It was the closest *Peanuts* fans would ever get to seeing her.

Those who said *Peanuts* had passed its prime were proved wrong in 1998 when a revival of *You're a Good Man, Charlie Brown* began a pre-Broadway run. The show was praised by critics in Detroit; St. Louis; Skokie, Illinois; and other cities. On February 4, 1999, it opened for the first time on Broadway. It was a huge hit and earned two Tony Awards for excellence in Broadway theater.

Another highlight in 1999 was the opening of a third Camp Snoopy. The setting was Cedar Point, a 364-acre amusement park in Sandusky, Ohio.

Schulz's 1997 comment that only an illness could make him stop drawing *Peanuts* became sadly true in November 1999 when he was diagnosed with colon cancer. During emergency surgery on his abdomen on November 16, Schulz suffered several small strokes. As a result, he could not see well from his left side, and he had trouble speaking.

What would become of *Peanuts*? "All of a sudden," said Schulz, "I'm in an ambulance, going to town and here I am. It's all over. I didn't mean for it to end like this, but it is. I have no choice, no choice whatsoever.

I don't know what to do. So I decided I might as well call it now."[19]

On December 14, Schulz announced that he wanted to spend as much time as possible with his family. After fifty years, the creator of *Peanuts* was going to retire. The last new daily *Peanuts* strip would run on January 3, 2000, and the last Sunday strip would be on February 13, 2000. Schulz planned to continue his work on new television specials and other projects.

People all over the world were saddened by the news of Schulz's retirement. Some publications invited readers to submit ideas for how *Peanuts* should end. Should Charlie Brown finally get to kick the football? Should Peppermint Patty finally get an A-plus? Should Schroeder tell Lucy he loves her? Or would it be better for the *Peanuts* gang to keep to the familiar patterns they had developed over five decades?

Schulz did not live to see his final comic strip in print. He died in his sleep around 9:45 the evening of February 12, 2000, just hours before newspapers carrying the last original *Peanuts* strip would be delivered to stores and homes around the world. At that time, *Peanuts* was featured in more than 2,600 newspapers in seventy-five countries.[20]

In his lifetime, Charles Schulz had created a total of 17,897 different *Peanuts* comic strips.[21]

And the last comic strip? It was a heartfelt, open letter to his readers. Surrounding the body of the letter were many of the familiar images that *Peanuts* readers had grown to know and love over the decades: Snoopy sitting atop his doghouse, Lucy in her psychiatric booth, Lucy pulling the football away yet again from

Charlie Brown. Schulz's letter read in part, "I have been grateful over the years for the loyalty of our editors and the wonderful support and love expressed to me by fans of the comic strip. Charlie Brown, Snoopy, Linus, Lucy . . . how can I ever forget them. . . ."[22]

Tributes to Schulz poured in from all over the world. Perhaps the most touching came from his fellow cartoonists: On Saturday, May 25, 2000, in New York City, Schulz was to have received the Milton Caniff Lifetime Achievement Award, the highest honor awarded by the National Cartoonists Society. His widow, Jeannie, accepted it in his place. That day, more than eighty of the world's best cartoonists devoted their comic strips to *Peanuts*. Paying tribute to Charles Schulz were *Garfield, Beetle Bailey, Cathy, For Better or For Worse, The Wizard of Id, Blondie, Hagar the Horrible*, and many other strips.

The honors continued. On May 17, 2001, the U.S. Postal Service unveiled a *Peanuts* stamp featuring Snoopy as the Flying Ace sitting atop his doghouse/plane. The stamp was planned to mark the fiftieth anniversary of the *Peanuts* comic strip.

That same spring, Worlds of Fun theme park in Kansas City, Missouri, opened a fourth Camp Snoopy.

On June 7, 2001, Jeannie Schulz accepted a Congressional Gold Medal on her late husband's behalf. This award, given by the president of the United States, is the country's highest civilian honor. Past honorees include George Washington, Rosa Parks, Pope John Paul II, and Mother Teresa.

In an earlier statement, released upon Schulz's death, President Bill Clinton had talked of "the many

"All I did was draw pictures," said Charles Schulz. But millions of fans around the world continue to treasure the wit and wisdom of Peanuts.

gifts he has given us all. . . . The hopeful and hapless Charlie Brown, the joyful Snoopy, the soulful Linus— even the 'crabby' Lucy—give voice, day after day, to what makes us human."[23]

In accordance with the Schulz family's wishes, no new *Peanuts* comic strips will ever be created by any other artist. But newspaper readers everywhere can still get their daily laugh with Charles Schulz and the *Peanuts* gang. Almost all the papers that carried *Peanuts* before Schulz's death are continuing the tradition by running reprints of classic *Peanuts* cartoons. *Peanuts* is a comic strip that is just too good to end.

Chronology

1922—Charles M. Schulz is born in Minneapolis, Minnesota, on November 26.

1929—Family moves briefly to Needles, California.

1937—Has first cartoon published, in Ripley's *Believe It or Not!*

1940—Graduates from high school.

1941—Begins courses at Federal Schools (later named Art Instruction Schools, Inc.).

1943—Drafted into U.S. Army for service in World War II.

1945—Takes lettering job at Timeless Topix; teaches at Art Instruction Schools, Inc.

1947—Begins drawing *Li'l Folks* for *St. Paul Pioneer Press*.

1948—First single-panel cartoon appears in *Saturday Evening Post*.

1950—*Peanuts* debuts in seven newspapers on October 2.

1951—Marries Joyce Halverson; family moves to Colorado Springs, Colorado.

1952—First *Peanuts* Sunday comic strip appears on January 6; Schroeder, Lucy, and Linus introduced; family moves back to Minnesota; first *Peanuts* book, titled *Peanuts*, is published.

1954—Pig-Pen is introduced; Linus is first seen with his security blanket.

1955—Wins Reuben Award from National Cartoonists Society.

1956—*Peanuts* is sold to its hundredth newspaper.

1958—Family moves to Sebastopol, California; *Peanuts* characters are merchandised for the first time.

1959—Sally Brown is born; the Great Pumpkin first mentioned.

1961—Frieda first appears.

1962—*Happiness Is a Warm Puppy* is published.

1963—5 is introduced.

1964—*The Gospel According to Peanuts* is published; Schulz wins another Reuben Award.

1965—*A Charlie Brown Christmas* first airs on television.

1966—Peppermint Patty enters the strip.

1967—*You're a Good Man, Charlie Brown* opens off-Broadway in New York City.

1968—Franklin is first seen.

1969—First *Peanuts* feature movie, *A Boy Named Charlie Brown*, is released; *Apollo X* takes "Charlie Brown" and "Snoopy" into outer space.

1970—Snoopy's bird friend is given the name Woodstock.

1971—Marcie is shown for the first time.

1972—Charles and Joyce Schulz divorce; Rerun enters *Peanuts* cast.

1973—Marries Jeannie Forsyth.

1975—Spike makes his first appearance.

1981—Schulz suffers a heart attack.

1983—*The Charlie Brown and Snoopy Show* premieres on television; Camp Snoopy opens at Knott's Berry Farm theme park in Buena Park, California.

1984—*Peanuts* sold to its two thousandth newspaper.

1988—*This Is America, Charlie Brown* is shown on television.

1990—Exhibit of Schulz's art opens in the Louvre in Paris, France.

1993—Charlie Brown hits a home run.

1997—Schulz takes his first vacation.

1998—Little red-haired girl appears for the only time, but in silhouette.

1999—*You're a Good Man, Charlie Brown* opens on Broadway; Schulz announces his retirement.

2000—Last daily strip runs on January 3; Schulz dies on February 12, just hours before his final *Peanuts* Sunday strip is published.

Chapter Notes

Chapter 1. Seven Newspapers

1. Charles M. Schulz, *Peanuts Jubilee: My Life and Art with Charlie Brown and Others* (New York: Holt, Rinehart and Winston, 1975), p. 30.

2. Ibid.

3. Rheta Grimsley Johnson, *Good Grief: The Story of Charles M. Schulz* (New York: Pharos Books, 1989), p. 25.

4. Ibid.

5. John Beck, "The Most Influential Strip," *The Press Democrat*, Santa Rosa, California, online edition, December 15, 1999, <http://www.pressdemo.com> (September 13, 2001).

Chapter 2. Needles, Sketches, and a Dog Named Spike

1. Richard Marschall, *America's Great Comic Strip Artists: From The Yellow Kid to Peanuts* (New York: Stewart, Tabori & Chang, 1997), p. 276.

2. "Charles M(onroe) Schulz," *Current Biography 1960* (New York: H. W. Wilson Co., 1960), p. 364.

3. Sarah Boxer, "Charles M. Schulz, 'Peanuts' Creator, Dies at 77," *The New York Times*, February 14, 2000, p. B8.

4. Rheta Grimsley Johnson, *Good Grief: The Story of Charles M. Schulz* (New York: Pharos Books, 1989), p. 32.

5. Russell D. Buhite and David W. Levy, *FDR's Fireside Chats* (New York: Penguin Books, 1993), p. 5.

6. Charles M. Schulz, *Around the World in 45 Years* (Kansas City, Mo.: Andrews and McMeel, 1994), p. 9.

7. Hugh Morrow, "The Success of an Utter Failure," *The Saturday Evening Post*, January 12, 1957, as reprinted in *Charles M. Schulz Conversations*, edited by M. Thomas Inge (Jackson, Miss.: University Press of Mississippi, 2000), p. 5.

8. Ibid.

9. "Charles Schulz: A Charlie Brown Life," *Biography*, written and directed by Randy Martin, Millenial Entertainment, Inc., and A&E Television Network, originally telecast December 25, 1995.

10. Lee Mendelson in association with Charles M. Schulz, *Charlie Brown & Charlie Schulz* (New York: Signet Books, 1971), frontispiece.

11. Morrow, p. 4.

12. Linda Witt, "The Soul of Peanuts: Will the Real Charlie Brown Please Stand Up?" *The Chicago Tribune*, December 22, 1985.

13. Charles M. Schulz, *Peanuts Jubilee: My Life and Art with Charlie Brown and Others* (New York: Holt, Rinehart and Winston, 1975), p. 13.

14. *Biography*.

15. Schulz, *Peanuts Jubilee*, p. 13.

16. Ibid., p. 12.

17. Mary Harrington Hall, "A Conversation with Charles Schulz or the Psychology of Simplicity," *Psychology Today*, January 1968, as reprinted in M. Thomas Inge, ed., *Charles M. Schulz Conversations* (Jackson: University Press of Mississippi, 2000), p. 53.

Chapter 3. ". . . Doing Something with Cartoons"

1. Charles M. Schulz, *Peanuts: A Golden Celebration* (New York: HarperCollins Publishers, 1999), p. 7.

2. Charles M. Schulz, *Peanuts Jubilee: My Life and Art with Charlie Brown and Others* (New York: Holt, Rinehart and Winston, 1975), p. 21.

3. Charles M. Schulz, *You Don't Look 35, Charlie Brown!* (New York: Holt, Rinehart and Winston, 1985).

4. "Charles Schulz: A Charlie Brown Life," *Biography*, written and directed by Randy Martin, Millenial Entertainment, Inc., and A&E Television Network, originally telecast December 25, 1995.

5. Linda Witt, "The Soul of Peanuts: Will the Real Charlie Brown Please Stand Up?" *The Chicago Tribune*, December 22, 1985.

6. Hugh Morrow, "The Success of an Utter Failure," *The Saturday Evening Post*, January 12, 1957, as reprinted in M. Thomas Inge, ed., *Charles M. Schulz Conversations* (Jackson: University Press of Mississippi, 2000), p. 12.

7. *Biography.*

8. Charles M. Schulz, *You Don't Look 35, Charlie Brown!* (New York: Holt, Rinehart and Winston, 1985).

9. Personal interview with Linus Maurer, October 26, 2000.

10. Ibid.

11. Ibid.

Chapter 4. From *Li'l Folks* to *Peanuts*

1. "Charles Schulz: A Charlie Brown Life," *Biography*, written and directed by Randy Martin, Millenial Entertainment, Inc., and A&E Television Network, originally telecast December 25, 1995.

2. Charles M. Schulz, *Peanuts Jubilee: My Life and Art with Charlie Brown and Others* (New York: Holt, Rinehart and Winston, 1975), p. 32.

3. Mary Harrington Hall, "A Conversation with Charles Schulz or The Psychology of Simplicity," *Psychology Today*, January 1968, as reprinted in M. Thomas Inge, ed., *Charles M. Schulz Conversations* (Jackson: University Press of Mississippi, 2000), p. 55.

4. Charles M. Schulz, *Peanuts Jubilee*, p. 30.

5. "Good Grief," *Time*, April 9, 1965, p. 82.

6. Gary Groth, "Schulz at 3 O'Clock in the Morning," *Comics Journal*, December 1977, as reprinted in M. Thomas Inge, ed., *Charles M. Schulz Conversations* (Jackson: University Press of Mississippi, 2000), p. 173.

7. *Biography.*

8. Ibid.

9. "You're a Good Man, Charles Schulz," *60 Minutes*, produced by Mary Murphy, telecast on CBS-TV, February 13, 2000.

10. Charles M. Schulz, *You Don't Look 35, Charlie Brown!* (New York: Holt, Rinehart and Winston, 1985).

11. Personal interview with Linus Maurer, October 26, 2000.

12. Charles M. Schulz, *Peanuts: A Golden Celebration* (New York: HarperCollins Publishers, 1999), p. 15.

Chapter 5. "Why Don't You Wish for Some Wings?"

1. Ann Commire, "Charles M(onroe) Schulz," *Something About the Author: Facts and Pictures about Contemporary Authors and Illustrators of Books for Young People* (Detroit: Gale Research Co., 1976), vol. 10, p. 140.

2. Charles M. Schulz, *Peanuts* (New York: Holt, Rinehart and Winston, 1952).

3. Ibid.

4. Ibid.

5. Ibid.

6. Ibid.

7. Sarah Boxer, "Charles M. Schulz, 'Peanuts' Creator, Dies at 77," *The New York Times*, February 14, 2000, p. B9.

8. Charles M. Schulz, *Good Grief, More Peanuts!* (New York: Holt, Rinehart and Winston, 1957).

9. United Media, <http://www.unitedmedia.com/comics/peanuts/f_profiles> (November 10, 2000).

10. Derrick Bang with Victor Lee, *50 Years of Happiness: A Tribute to Charles M. Schulz* (Davis, Calif.: Peanuts Collectors Club, Inc., 1999).

11. Ibid.

12. Charles M. Schulz, *Peanuts Jubilee: My Life and Art with Charlie Brown and Others* (New York: Holt, Rinehart and Winston, 1975), p. 83.

Chapter 6. Flying Kites and Selling Cars

1. United Media, <http://www.unitedmedia.com/comics/peanuts/f_profiles> (November 10, 2000).

2. Hugh Morrow, "The Success of an Utter Failure," *The Saturday Evening Post*, January 12, 1957, as reprinted in M. Thomas Inge, ed., *Charles M. Schulz Conversations* (Jackson: University Press of Mississippi, 2000), p. 11.

3. Richard Marschall, *America's Great Comic Strip Artists: From the Yellow Kid to Peanuts* (New York: Stewart, Tabori & Chang, 1997), p. 278.

4. Personal interview with Dale Hale, November 10, 2000.

5. Ibid.

6. "Child's Garden of Reverses," *Time*, March 3, 1958, p. 58.

7. Personal interview with Craig Schulz, October 16, 2000.

8. Charles M. Schulz, *But We Love You, Charlie Brown* (New York: Holt, Rinehart and Winston, 1959).

9. Rheta Grimsley Johnson, *Good Grief: The Story of Charles M. Schulz* (New York: Pharos Books, 1989), p. 77.

10. Personal interview with Craig Schulz, August 31, 2001.

11. Personal interview with Cathy Guisewite, October 5, 2001.

12. "Charles M(onroe) Schulz," *Current Biography 1960* (New York: H. W. Wilson Co., 1960), p. 364.

13. Gaye LeBaron. "Drawn to His Trade," *The Press Democrat*, Santa Rosa, Calif., November 23, 1997, <www.pressdemo.com/news/schulz> (June 9, 2000).

14. Charles M. Schulz, *Go Fly a Kite, Charlie Brown* (New York: Holt, Rinehart and Winston, 1960).

15. Ibid.

16. Ibid.

17. Personal interview with Bill Melendez, November 2, 2000.

18. Ibid.

19. Ibid.

20. Charles M. Schulz, *It's a Dog's Life, Charlie Brown* (New York: Holt, Rinehart and Winston, 1962).

Chapter 7. Charlie Brown: Television Star

1. Charles M. Schulz, *Peanuts Jubilee: My Life and Art with Charlie Brown and Others* (New York: Holt, Rinehart and Winston, 1975), p. 86.

2. "You're a Good Man, Charles Schulz," *60 Minutes*, produced by Mary Murphy, telecast on CBS-TV, February 13, 2000.

3. Personal interview with Lynn Johnston, October 27, 2000.

4. Charles M. Schulz, *It's a Dog's Life, Charlie Brown* (New York: Holt, Rinehart and Winston, 1962).

5. "Good Grief: Curly Hair," *Newsweek*, March 6, 1961, p. 68.

6. Schulz, *It's a Dog's Life, Charlie Brown.*

7. Ibid.

8. Personal interview with Amy Johnson, October 27, 2000.

9. Charles M. Schulz, *As You Like It, Charlie Brown* (New York: Holt, Rinehart and Winston, 1964).

10. Personal interview with Amy Johnson, October 27, 2000.

11. "On Happiness," *Life*, December 14, 1962, p. 23.

12. Charles M. Schulz, *Happiness Is a Warm Puppy* (San Francisco: Determined Productions, 1962).

13. Schulz, *As You Like It, Charlie Brown.*

14. Ibid.

15. Lee Mendelson, *A Charlie Brown Christmas: The Making of a Tradition* (New York: HarperCollins Publishers, 2000), p. 14.

16. Ibid., p. 15.

17. Personal interview with Bill Melendez, November 2, 2000.

18. Ibid.

19. Personal interview with Monte Schulz, October 29, 2000.

20. Mendelson, p. 31.

21. Personal interview with Bill Melendez, November 2, 2000.

Chapter 8. The New Neighborhood

1. Charles M. Schulz, *Peanuts: A Golden Celebration* (New York: HarperCollins Publishers, 1999), p. 66.

2. Ibid.

3. Lee Mendelson, *Happy Birthday, Charlie Brown* (New York: Random House, 1979), p. 94.

4. Charles M. Schulz, *The Unsinkable Charlie Brown* (New York: Holt, Rinehart and Winston, 1967).

5. Personal interview with Bill Melendez, November 2, 2000.

6. Joel Whitburn, *The Billboard Book of Top 40 Hits* (New York: Billboard Productions, 1996), p. 523.

7. Personal interview with Craig Schulz, October 16, 2000.

8. Whitburn, p. 563.

9. Personal interview with Craig Schulz, October 16, 2000.

10. Personal interview with Clark Gesner, November 11, 2000.

11. Ibid.

12. Ibid.

13. Charles M. Schulz, *You're Something Else, Charlie Brown* (New York: Holt, Rinehart and Winston, 1968).

14. Jud Hurd, "Cartoonist Profiles: Charles Schulz," *Cartoonist Profiles*, December, 1979, as reprinted in M. Thomas Inge, ed., *Charles M. Schulz Conversations* (Jackson: University Press of Mississippi, 2000), p. 99.

15. "Charles Schulz: A Charlie Brown Life," *Biography*, written and directed by Randy Martin, Millenial Entertainment, Inc., and A&E Television Network, originally telecast December 25, 1995.

16. Charles M. Schulz, *Charlie Brown, Snoopy and Me* (New York: Fawcett Columbine, 1980), p. 41.

17. Cynthia Gorney, "The Peanuts Progenitor," *The Washington Post*, October 2, 1985, p. D2.

18. *Biography*.

Chapter 9. "What Do You Think Security Is?"

1. Barnaby Conrad, "You're a Good Man, Charlie Schulz," *The New York Times Magazine*, April 16, 1967, p. 33.

2. Personal interview with Amy Johnson, October 16, 2001.

3. Personal interview with Amy Johnson, October 27, 2000.

4. Ibid.

5. Personal interview with Craig Schulz, October 16, 2000.

6. Charles M. Schulz, *Thompson Is in Trouble, Charlie Brown* (New York: Holt, Rinehart and Winston, 1973).

7. Personal interview with Monte Schulz, October 29, 2000.

8. Personal interview with Amy Johnson, October 30, 2000.

9. Charles M. Schulz, *You've Come a Long Way, Charlie Brown* (New York: Holt, Rinehart and Winston, 1971).

10. Personal interview with Amy Johnson, October 30, 2000.

11. Charles M. Schulz, *You've Come a Long Way, Charlie Brown.*

12. Personal interview with Amy Johnson, October 30, 2000.

13. Charles M. Schulz, *Thompson Is in Trouble, Charlie Brown.*

Chapter 10. Success, Failure, and a Desert Rat

1. Charles M. Schulz, *Peanuts: A Golden Celebration* (New York: HarperCollins Publishers, 1999), p. 103.

2. Personal interview with Monte Schulz, October 29, 2000.

3. Charles M. Schulz, *You Don't Look 35, Charlie Brown!* (New York: Holt, Rinehart and Winston, 1985.

4. Personal interview with Jill Schulz Transki, October 27, 2000.

5. Personal interview with Monte Schulz, October 29, 2000.

6. Charles M. Schulz, *Peanuts: A Golden Celebration*, p. 254.

7. Giovanni Trimboli, *Charles M. Schulz: 40 Years of Life and Art* (New York: Pharos Books, 1990), p. 35.

8. Personal interview with Bill Melendez, November 2, 2000.

9. Rheta Grimsley Johnson, *Good Grief: The Story of Charles M. Schulz* (New York: Pharos Books, 1989), p. 196.

10. Ibid.

11. Personal interview with Bill Melendez, November 2, 2000.

12. Personal interview with Jill Schulz Transki, October 27, 2000.

Chapter 11. "You?!"

1. Personal interview with Amy Lago, October 24, 2000.

2. Ibid.

3. Ibid.

4. Personal interview with Cathy Guisewite, November 3, 2000.

5. Charles M. Schulz, *Peanuts: A Golden Celebration* (New York: HarperCollins Publishers, 1999), p. 194.

6. Charles M. Schulz, *Around the World in 45 Years* (Kansas City, Mo.: Andrews and McMeel, 1994), p. 71.

7. Ibid.

8. Ibid.

9. "You're a Good Man, Charles Schulz," *60 Minutes*, produced by Mary Murphy, telecast on CBS-TV February 13, 2000.

10. Personal interview with Lynn Johnston, October 27, 2000.

11. Personal interview with Cathy Guisewite, November 3, 2000.

12. Rheta Grimsley Johnson, *Good Grief: The Story of Charles M. Schulz* (New York: Pharos Books, 1989), p. 161.

13. Ibid., p. 157.

14. Personal interview with Lynn Johnston, October 27, 2000.

15. Personal interview with Cathy Guisewite, November 3, 2000.

16. Personal interview with Lynn Johnston, October 27, 2000.

17. Personal interview with Craig Schulz, October 16, 2000.

18. Gaye LeBaron, "Drawn to His Trade," *The Press Democrat*, Santa Rosa, Calif., November 23, 1997, <www.pressdemo.com/news/schulz> June 9, 2000.

19. Meg McConahey, "Cancer Fight Forces Abrupt End to 50-Year-Old Strip," *The Press Democrat*, Santa Rosa, Calif., December 15, 1999, online archives, <www.pressdemo.com> (September 13, 2001).

20. Mary Ann Lickteig, "Farewell, Charlie Brown," Associated Press, <ABCNews.com> (February 13, 2000).

21. Derrick Bang, "Peanuts at 50: Fast Facts," *The Davis [California] Enterprise*, weekend section, September 28, 2000, p. 11.

22. *Keene [New Hampshire] Sentinel*, Sunday comics page, February 13, 2000.

23. Eulogy by President Bill Clinton, February 13, 2000, <http://peanutscollectorclub.com/eulogy.html> (August 13, 2001).

Further Reading

Bang, Derrick, with Victor Lee. *50 Years of Happiness: A Tribute to Charles M. Schulz.* Davis, Calif.: Peanuts Collectors Club, Inc., 1999.

Goulart, Ron. *The Great Comic Book Artists.* New York: St. Martin's Press. Vol. 1, 1986. Vol. 2, 1989.

Johnson, Rheta Grimsley. *Good Grief: The Story of Charles M. Schulz.* New York: Pharos Books, 1989.

Kidd, Chip, with photos by Geoff Spear. *Peanuts: The Art of Charles M. Schulz.* New York: Pantheon Books, 2001.

Marschall, Richard. *America's Great Comic Strip Artists: From the Yellow Kid to Peanuts.* New York: Stewart, Tabori & Chang, 1997.

Mendelson, Lee, with reflections by Bill Melendez. *A Charlie Brown Christmas: The Making of a Tradition.* New York: HarperCollins Publishers, 2000.

Mendelson, Lee, in association with Charles M. Schulz. *Happy Birthday, Charlie Brown.* New York: Random House, 1979.

Robinson, Jerry. *The Comics: An Illustrated History of Comic Strip Art.* New York: Putnam, 1974.

Schulz, Charles M., *Around the World in 45 Years.* Kansas City, Mo.: Andrews and McMeel, 1994.

———. *Peanuts: A Golden Celebration.* New York: HarperCollins Publishers, 1999.

————. *Peanuts Jubilee: My Life and Art with Charlie Brown and Others.* New York: Holt, Rinehart and Winston, 1975.

————. *You Don't Look 35, Charlie Brown!* New York: Holt, Rinehart and Winston, 1985.

Schulz, Charles M., and R. Smith Kiliper. *Charlie Brown, Snoopy and Me.* New York: Fawcett Columbine, 1980.

Scott, Elaine, with photographs by Margaret Miller. *Funny Papers: Behind the Scenes of the Comics.* New York: Morrow Junior Books, 1993.

Trimboli, Giovanni. *Charles M. Schulz: 40 Years of Life and Art.* New York: Pharos Books, 1990.

Internet Addresses

Charles M. Schulz Museum
This museum in Santa Rosa, California, is devoted to all things relating to Peanuts.
<http://www.charlesmschulzmuseum.org/>

United Media's "Home of Peanuts on the Web"
Comic strips, biography, timeline, and more.
<http://www.snoopy.com/>

Peanuts Collector Club
Everything from facts to newspaper articles.
<http://www.peanutscollectorclub.com/>

International Museum of Cartoon Art
Information about cartoonists worldwide.
<http://www.cartoon.org/>

Scott's Peanuts Animation and Reprints page
A guide to the Peanuts gang on television, film, and video.
<http://web.mit.edu/smcguire/www/peanuts.html>

Index

Page numbers for photographs and comic strips are in **boldface** type.